OFFBE

A Practical Guide to Pop and Jazz for GCSE

Richard Crozier

Bell & Hyman

First published in 1987 by
BELL & HYMAN
An imprint of Unwin Hyman Limited
Denmark House, 37/39 Queen Elizabeth Street
London SE1 2QB

British Library Cataloguing in Publication Data
Crozier, Richard
    Offbeat: a practical guide to pop & jazz for GCSE.
    1. Music, Popular (Songs, etc.) – History and
    criticism
    I. Title
    780′.42   ML3470
    ISBN 0 7135 2751 X

Designed by Snap Graphics
Music setting by Toppan Scan-Note Printing Co.
Typeset by Tradespools Ltd, Frome, Somerset
Printed in Great Britain by Scotprint Ltd, Musselburgh

Contents

Acknowledgements

The publishers would like to thank the following for permission to reproduce material in their copyright:

For an extract from 'One hand, one heart' from *West Side Story*, music by Leonard Bernstein, © 1957 by Leonard Bernstein and Stephen Sondheim, reproduced by kind permission of Campbell Connelly & Co. Ltd, 8/9 Frith Street, London W1V 5TZ; EMI Music Publishing Ltd and International Music Publications for an extract from 'We are the Champions', words and music by Freddie Mercury, © 1977 Queen Music Ltd; Intersong Music Limited for an extract from 'Flashdance', words by Keith Forsey and Irene Cara, music by Giogio Moroder; Dick James Music Ltd, 45 Berkeley Square, London W1X 5DB, for an extract from 'Can't Smile Without You' by Chris Arnold, David Martin and Geoff Morrow, © 1975 Dick James Music; extract from 'Superstition' by Stevie Wonder, © 1972 Jobete Music Company Inc. and Black Bull Music Inc., 6255 Sunset Boulevard, Los Angeles, California 90028, USA, Jobete Music (UK) Ltd/Black Bull Music, Tudor House, 35 Gresse Street, London W1P 1PN for UK and Eire; Mills Music Inc for an extract from the Chorus of 'It don't mean a thing' by Duke Ellington and Irving Mills, © 1932 by Mills Music Inc., Copyright renewed 1960; extract from 'Lullaby of Birdland' (George Shearing/George David Weiss), © 1952, 1953, 1954 by Adam R. Levy and Father Ent. Inc., Planetary-Nom (London) Ltd, 45 Berkeley Square, London W1X 5DB. For British Commonwealth (excluding Canada and Australasia) also for Republic of Ireland; Proctor & Gamble for the melody line from the Fairy Liquid advertisement; 'When I'm 64' John Lennon/Paul McCartney, © 1969 Northern Songs under licence to SBK Songs, 3–5 Rathbone Place, London W1P 4AA

Picture credits
Thanks are due to the following who supplied copyright material:

Air Studios, p.81; Barnaby's Picture Library, pp. 32 (top right), 71 (top left, top centre, top right, centre right, bottom right, bottom centre, centre left), 73 (top left); BBC Hulton Picture Library, p.30; Chappell Music, p.23; Decca Record Company Ltd, p.67; Deuce Music, p.53 (lower left); Dolby Laboratories, p.62 (bottom); Erica Echenberg, p.73 (bottom left); EMI records, pp.20 (top), 66; *Exchange & Mart*, p.31; Paul Finch, p.55 (top centre); Harold Holt, p. 53 (centre left, top right); Ibbs & Tillett, p.53 (centre right); Max Jones, pp.8, 10 (bottom right), 21, 22; London Features International, pp.33 (bottom left), 73 (right), 79 (bottom right); N M Mander, p.55 (centre right); Mansell Collection, p.23 (bottom left); Morley Galleries, p. 55 (top right, bottom right, centre left); R. S. Wherry, B.Sc., Head of Norton Hill School, Midsomer Norton, Bath, p.75; Popperfoto, pp.32 (left), 33 (top right, bottom right), 53 (left), 70, 79 (bottom left and right, second left); Rank Hovis, p.76; RarePic Collection, pp.33 (top left), 53 (lower right); David Redfern, pp.24, 32 (bottom right), 33 (centre right), 66, 67, 71 (bottom left, centre), 72 (all), 78 (all), 79 (top left, top centre, top right, centre right, centre left); Brian Rust, pp.10 (top; bottom left), 11; Sony (UK), pp.62 (top), 63; Steinway & Sons, p.55 (centre); Yamaha-Kemble Music (UK), p.55 (top left; bottom centre.)

Introduction

This book is intended for use by GCSE pupils – starting in Years 3 and 4, and extending into the 5th year. It is concerned with two aspects of musical history: Recording, and Pop Music, with closely related practical work. It can be used by a pupil with limited musical knowledge, but hopefully by the third year of secondary school all pupils will have some experience of practical music making in addition to their acquired musical knowledge.

Most of the practical work should be tackled by small groups of pupils, i.e. 4–6 per group, but if resources permit group size can be reduced. My experience of using the material in this book tells me that small classrooms with five or six groups working simultaneously are possible, and that children are far less distracted by the noise of others than teachers are. Headphones for electronic keyboards are clearly a good investment!

In the middle of the book is a reference section which will be used in conjunction with many of the practical sections. Written work should rarely, if ever, be done in isolation; it should be combined with practical work – perhaps recorded on tape or video – and should be seen as part of a whole. Teachers and pupils will benefit from working together to use the book and should cross-refer from section to section, particularly on the practical work. At the back of the book is an assessment page (which may be photocopied), of which both pupil and teacher can keep a copy.

Richard Crozier

Some encouragement for pupils

Many people would say that the best thing about music is actually playing it, singing it, or composing it. Your teacher can easily play you examples of all the different styles of composition mentioned in this book but you'll understand about them much better if you try to compose in them, or play in them yourself. You will also find that the practical bits do connect up with the historical bits, but it's up to you and your teacher to decide in which order to tackle things. The diagram below should help to show you how things fit together. The most important thing that this book is going to try to do is to make you become a composer and performer (even if you're not a very good one!), in just the same way that your art, woodwork, metalwork, pottery, or cookery lessons help you to gain skills in the practical sides of those subjects. You'll soon find out, if you haven't already, that a bit of basic knowledge goes a long way in music, so don't put off the 'rudiments' sections altogether – use them as often as you need to. The words in **bold** type through the book are explained in the Glossary, which is on pages 38–41.

Music is an art of communication. The composer has to communicate with: (a) the person who wants to perform his music – usually by means of writing it down in an efficient manner, and (b) the person who listens to his music. You may become more skilful as a composer, performer or listener, but you will have some ability at all three – make the most of it! Good luck!

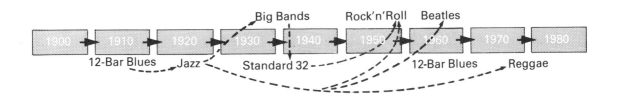

Popular music in Britain at the beginning of this century

King Oliver's Dixie Syncopators. This photograph, taken in the mid-1920s, shows the established line-up of instruments in the early dance bands.

AMERICAN INFLUENCE, 1900–1920

It is difficult to sort out truth from fiction in the early years of 'popular music'. Perhaps one reason for this is the fact that no one wishes to associate themselves with a style or idea that didn't catch on, while everyone is willing to lay claim to an idea that, perhaps later, captured everyone's imagination.

The year 1910 seems to be the generally accepted date for the beginning of dance bands.

The common line-up was:

2 or more brass instruments
2 or more saxophones (**doubling**)
piano ⎫
banjo ⎬ rhythm section
drums ⎭
plus (sometimes) brass bass
violin – the lead instrument

Dance music played by these bands depended on **syncopation** for its interest, i.e. putting the accent on notes that don't come at the beginning of the bar. Its direct historical links were with poor Black Americans, the descendants of the slaves, and the particular musical forms used were those such as the **blues**, **ragtime**, **cakewalk**, etc. The strong two-in-a-bar feel of these styles contributed to the overall unity of the style that was developing. This style gradually achieved wide acceptance and near-respectability, via the **minstrel shows** and the increasingly common practice of adding band parts to the publication of the sheet music. Another important factor was the developing popularity of the **Foxtrot**, a new ballroom dance that existed in a variety of disguises, including the **Horsetrot** and the **Fishwalk**. The spread of the foxtrot with its firm two-beat rhythm was due in no small way to the **gramophone**, which allowed many people to practise their dance steps at home, and many more to become familiar with its sound.

Irene and Vernon Castle began to demonstrate the new dance steps, like the foxtrot, in 1914 and they sparked off a society dance craze centred around the foxtrot. When the USA entered World War One an American called **James Europe** toured Western Europe with his band and was highly acclaimed. With the impetus of people like the Castles and bands like that of James Europe, and the feelings and desires promoted by the frustrations and humiliations of the First World War a number of changes in social patterns began to develop across the USA. Dance-halls gradually acquired an air of respectability, particularly in the view of younger people and along with this professional bands, rather than the amateur or semi-professional bands, began to provide music in the newly opened ballrooms that were established in better class hotels.

Gradually these musical developments spread from the USA to Western Europe, taking until about 1940 to reach the USSR. Britain, perhaps because it is the nearest country, and because of the absence of a language barrier, remained a close second to the USA in the spread of these new styles of popular music.

Compare this early record label with one of your own.

Slaves shipped from Africa to the USA brought with them their music – melancholy songs, spirituals and strong syncopated rhythm. The map shows how the music spread northwards from New Orleans and eventually reached Western Europe.

CAN YOU?

1 Find relations or others who know how to do dances like the foxtrot. Can they show you how to do them?
2 Find out what these dances were and make a drawing to show the steps for the foxtrot.
3 Explain why you think fashion connects with music.
4 Compare the line up of a 1910 dance band with that of a modern pop group.
5 Draw a dancing couple of: (a) then, and (b) today, to demonstrate their clothing and style.

TALKING POINT

1 With a group of friends, discuss and compare the musical scene for a person of your age in 1910 with today's musical scene. Was one or the other better off – if so, why?
2 What effect did improved communications have on the development of musical styles and taste between 1900 and 1920? What was the result of this improvement in everyday terms?

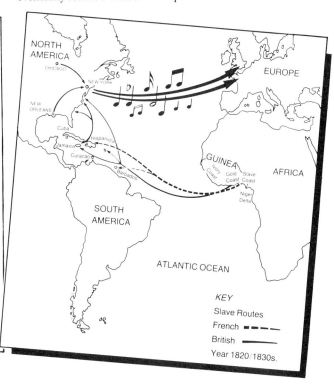

Paul Whiteman and his band, 1921.

THE 1920s

The chief factor in the growth of popular music in the 1920s was the development of radio. This had been somewhat overshadowed in the first twenty years of the century by the gramophone, but technological development enabled radio sets to be mass-produced cheaply by the end of the First World War. In the USA sales figures for radios soared from $60 million in 1922 to over $800 million by 1930. Radio was organized locally and was dependent upon advertising sponsorship for its success. Gradually, particular bands became associated with certain sponsors and thus assured themselves of regular air-time and a wide audience. The 1920s also witnessed the continuing growth of dance-halls as dancing gradually became more popular and respectable, and many hotels opened ballrooms and employed resident bands.

To the American public the 'King of Jazz' in the 1920s was **Paul Whiteman**, born in 1890. He received a classical musical training and started his career playing in American symphony orchestras.

His change of musical direction began during the First World War (1914–1918) when he organized one of the American Navy bands and used this 40-piece band to try out his arrangements of 'symphonic jazz'. In 1924, Whiteman gave a concert at the Aeolian Hall in New York, leading a 23-piece orchestra in a programme entitled 'An Experiment in Modern Music' which included **George Gershwin** at the piano playing his new composition 'Rhapsody in Blue'. The audience included the famous violinist **Heifetz** and the great Russian composer **Stravinsky**, and was a great success. Whiteman initially forbade his musicians to depart from the written notes so it could be argued that they were not playing jazz at all. But in 1927 he changed his views on this and employed 'genuine' jazz musicians in the band and actively encouraged them to play solos. It is interesting to note that 'jazzers' such as **Bix Beiderbecke** found much of the Whiteman music difficult to play because they were more accustomed to improvising and were less well trained in the art of sight reading – something in which non-jazz musicians tend to specialize.

Bix Beiderbecke.

Ambrose and his May Fair Hotel Orchestra recording in 1929.

In the closing years of the 1920s, Whiteman led his most impressive band which included a number of gifted soloists – Beiderbecke, **Eddie Lang**, the **Dorsey brothers** – and used **Ferd Grofe** to write many of his arrangements. At the height of his success Whiteman lived the part of the show-biz star – he weighed over twenty stone and was a jovial man who enjoyed high living. America in the 1920s produced a great many bands: **Jean Goldkette, Coon Sanders Nighthawks, Fred Waring, the Ipana Troubadours, the California Ramblers, the Benson Orchestra of Chicago**, and lots of others.

When looking at any period of history and its music, it is important to remember all the things which may influence the composition of music and the way in which it is played. By the end of the 1920s, both in America and in Great Britain, there were major financial problems; this was a period of strikes and financial depression with large numbers of people unemployed. The future of the bands seemed very uncertain, and it looked as if band-leaders would find it impossible to keep such large groups of musicians together. Yet, within a few years, the **Big Band** era dawned.

Wilbur C. Sweatman's Original Jazz Band.

Dance Records

This page from a record list of 1917 shows the popularity of the early jazz bands.

The Original Dixieland Jass Band

SPELL it Jass, Jas, Jaz or Jazz—nothing can spoil a Jass band. Some say the Jass band originated in Chicago. Chicago says it comes from San Francisco—San Francisco being away off across the continent. Anyway, a Jass band is the newest thing in the cabarets, adding greatly to the hilarity thereof.

They say the first instrument of the first Jass band was an empty lard can, by humming into which, sounds were produced resembling those of a saxophone with the croup. Since then the Jass band has grown in size and ferocity, and only

---

CAN YOU?

1 Find any examples of 1920s music on records at your home or at relations'.
2 Attempt to explain how musical fashions change and why, in the 1920s in America, a particular kind of band became popular.
3 Explain why Paul Whiteman is considered important by students of musical history.

TALKING POINT

1 Why was Paul Whiteman attractive to the general public? Would he attract as much publicity today?
2 How did the financial situation of the late 1920s directly or indirectly affect people's musical tastes and other things?

Jazz improvisation

Improvisation is a word used in connection with music as well as many other things and it means 'to make it up as you go along'. It's the essential element in jazz but you can also improvise in other musical styles as well. This practical section will help you to understand how players in a band like Paul Whiteman's might have worked. Some jazz musicians will argue that you cannot learn to improvise, you just have to get up and do it; but, working on the assumption that most people will benefit from a little help, here are some ideas.

METHOD 1

This method probably explains how a great many people have actually learned to improvise, and that is by listening to others playing and then memorizing their phrases. So, here are some standard patterns that you can copy, fitting them in when they sound OK, and then building and expanding. Try playing each pattern and if possible use others in your group to play the accompanying chords shown underneath each phrase.

Remember that each pattern belongs to a particular chord – its name is printed underneath each bar.

The chords used on this page:

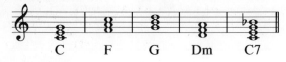

METHOD 2

This is probably more difficult and will be slower to provide good results, but is a direct link with the method that jazz musicians use. It involves reading ahead and being able to read and interpret the **chord signs** as given.

By the way, in the middle of the book you'll find a number of sections to help you with problems like understanding how chords work. You should refer to those sections as often as you need to – they're there to help you to get on quickly without having to ask. All the words shown in **bold** are explained in the glossary which is also in the middle of the book.

First play one note – say the **tonic** from each chord:

then add the third and fifth:

then add passing notes in-between:

METHOD 3

This is a sophisticated combination of the first two methods and, yes, it's a little more difficult. You need to read the chord symbols and be able to imagine or hear the sounds in your head but, of course, in advance of the notes that you're actually going to play. You can then put phrases together which will fit in neatly and if you're clever enough, you can recognize a familiar chord pattern and perhaps put in a quotation from another tune which has the same chord pattern.

The chords used on this page:

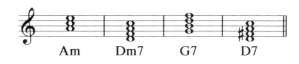

RHYTHMIC IMPROVISATION

Successful improvisation only comes with a lot of practice, so don't despair – keep coming back to this section and don't be afraid to try things out! If you find that getting a workable melody or logical-sounding pattern of notes is difficult, you may prefer to stick to rhythmic figures based on the given chords. Try some of these.

13

The 12-bar blues (1)

Blues is the term given to a pattern of harmony. It can be 8, 12, or 16 bars long and developed from the tradition of vocal music that existed in the southern states of the USA towards the end of the last century.

When you are familiar with the pattern that makes up a 12-bar blues, you can make up – improvise – your own tunes and, of course, words.

By the way, bar 12 here is shown as C major – which allows you to go back to the beginning and play it again. When you finally end, use a chord of F major in bar 12.

12-BAR BLUES IN F MAJOR

Note the **key signature** of one flat – B♭ for F major – so all the other Bs must be played as B♭.

The chords as shown above provide the 'backing'. Try this 12 bar, adding as many parts as you can.

1 Guitar (rhythm) – 4 **strums** to a bar ////

2 Piano – 4 chords to a bar, like the guitar part.
   Use one or two players, depending on how skilled you are.

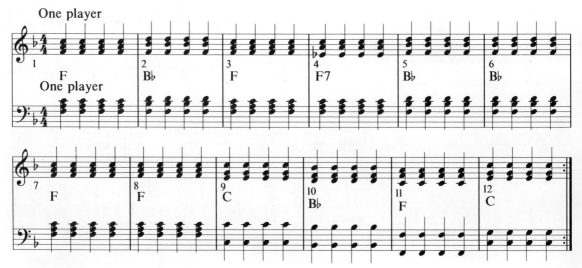

3 Easy piano

4 The tune – voices, flute, recorders, violins, glocks

Sing the blues, ev' - ry day, sing the blues right now. If you want to sing the blues, it's ea - sy. Yeah!

5 Glocks 1 and 2

6 Glocks 3 and 4   P.S. Glock 3 is fairly easy!

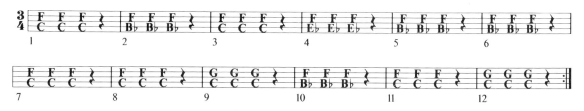

7 Untuned percussion   ✗ means play it again!

8 Easy double-bass

In the double-bass part, the note can be played
twice in each bar, like this:

etc.

9 Snare drum

etc.

10 B♭ instruments
You decide – 1 × one-beat note, and 3 one-
beat rests per bar, or 4 one-beat notes in each
bar.

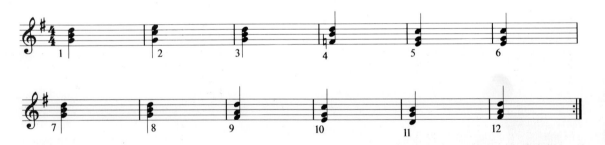

11 Riffs
Use this rhythm: do-be do-be do-wah
                1   2   3   4

and make up your own notes;

or try this rhythm: do   do-be do-wah
              1 2 3 4 1   2   3   4

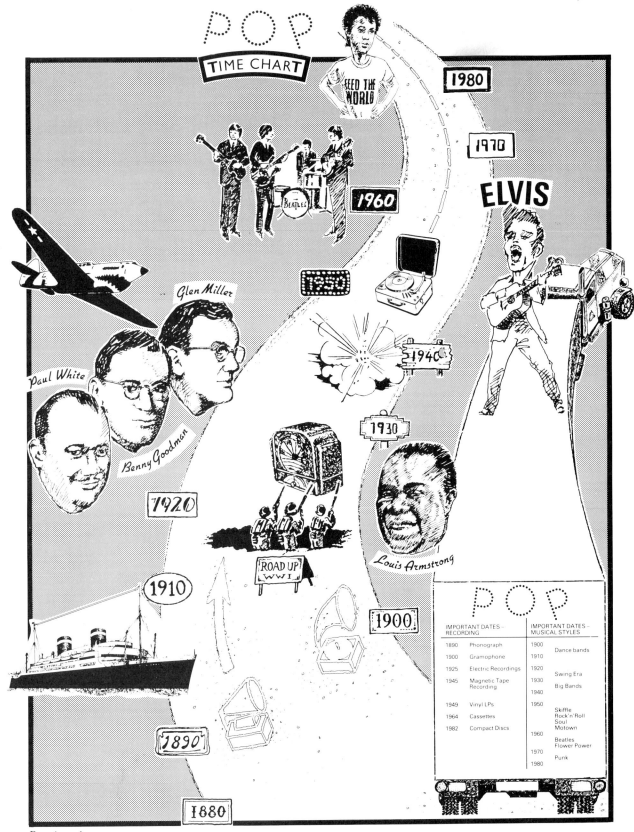

Pop time chart.

Riffs and easy figures

The word 'riff' means a repeated musical pattern – usually short. It's used a lot in jazz and also in pop. **'Classical'** musicians talk about **ostinato** (not from British Leyland!) and mean much the same thing.

Here are some examples you can play on a keyboard or glock, or clarinet, flute, etc. If you're not sure about these signs: ♭ ♯ ♮ turn to the Rudiments section for help.

> means 'accent' this beat

A riff for a 12-bar blues (boogie feel)

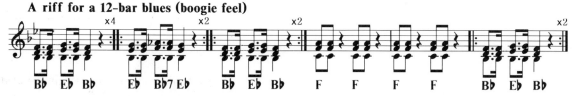

Underneath each riff is the chord that goes with it. So, if you have someone who can play chords on a guitar or piano (keyboard), or if you can share the notes of the chords out between a few instruments, you should find that you can quickly create an effective musical sound – and you'll recognize that some pop songs only use a much repeated riff.

Some pop musicians have used exciting bass riffs over which they can improvise and also carry a tune. Take, for example, this song by **Stevie Wonder**:

Have a rest for a minuet – think of some current pop songs that contain riffs or easy figures, such as those below. Then you can have a go at composing some of your own.

From 'Superstition' by Stevie Wonder
(arranged for windband)

COMPOSING RIFFS

Like all other composition, work hard – to a method – don't wait for inspiration. Don't try to be too clever – be simple. Begin, perhaps, by choosing notes from just one or two chords, for example:

C $^{G}_{E}$$_{C}$ and F $^{C}_{A}$$_{F}$ using occasional in-between notes.

Set yourself a steady beat – usually 4 per bar, and use any melody instrument to work with. Judge success by singability! – don't be shy.

COMPOSING EASY FIGURES

It will be even harder to be original in this section. Begin by trying to copy some memorable figures from records that you listen to now.

There's nothing mysterious about the name 'easy figures' – that's exactly what they are. Yes, they can be riffs or might just be the kind of thing that you recognize from pop, light music generally and the sort of thing that, if you can play them, people will say, 'Ooh, that sounds just like . . .'.

Bass

The other figures will sound good on any instrument.

The same figure for treble clef readers:

Keyboard

Acoustic and electrical recording

The development of popular music is closely linked with the history of recorded sound and wireless. It is a difficult point to understand, and some of the information which follows will be difficult to believe, but early recording was an entirely mechanical, **acoustic** process and electricity wasn't used at all.

Look at this photograph which shows the English composer and conductor **Edward Elgar** in a 'recording studio' belonging to 'The Gramophone Company' in 1915. Although the players may have been bunched together for the photograph, the fact is that they had to be as close as possible to the horn which is sticking out at the right hand side, because the sounds from their instruments produced sound waves which are concentrated by the shape of the horn.

Elgar, conducting his first recording at City Road, London (late 1914 or early 1915).

In 1925 the first electrical recordings were made, using a **microphone** to pick up the sounds, and this heralded the beginning of a period of development in the improvement of sound quality.

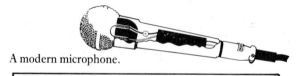

A modern microphone.

An early gramophone horn.

At the narrow end of the horn is a diaphram – a thin piece of metal which vibrates because of the sounds coming into the horn. This diaphram is connected to a needle which cuts the groove in the wax cylinder or disc. There were, of course, many problems: background noise was easily picked up and quieter instruments could not be heard unless they were placed near to the horn – look at the violins in the photograph.

Balance between solo and accompaniment was difficult to attain, as was the balance between voice and instruments, and upright pianos were often used because they could be more easily raised above floor level so as to be nearer to the horn's opening.

CAN YOU?

1 Make a sketch drawing of a recording studio before 1925.
2 Imagine the early days of recording and act out a scene in a recording studio.
3 Is there anywhere you can listen to a 78 r.p.m. recording (at home, in school) and compare the sound quality with a modern recording?

TALKING POINT

1 How many musicians are there in the Elgar photograph?
2 Can you work out who is playing what in that photo?
3 Is their clothing in any way remarkable?
4 Do you think that as recordings became more popular, composers would write for the number of players that would fit into a recording studio?
5 Find out how many members of staff know anything about Elgar.

Big bands

Big Bands are exactly what their name suggests, and the photo below shows one led by Black American Duke Ellington in 1933.

Although the numbers varied, the Big Bands all had the following sections:

①Reeds ②Trumpets ③Trombones ④Rhythm

Note the bass saxophone.

They developed in the 1920s and became especially popular in the 1930s and early 1940s. One of the most famous band-leaders was United States Air Force Officer **Glenn Miller**. Some of the 1920s' bands even included a string section, like this one (below) led by Paul Whiteman and so the Big Bands give us a direct link with the orchestra of the 1880s and 1890s that played 'light' music but had started to use saxophones.

TALKING POINT

Look at the Time Chart on page 17 and you can see how the Big Band or Swing Band era grew out of the 1920s' passion for jazz. It might be said that young people in the 1930s were looking for something that would be theirs and theirs alone – something that their parents would disapprove of – and swing music filled this gap. You can compare this with what has happened between 1950 and 1980 – the development of rock music. Compare your parents' reaction to a lot of today's pop music with that of parents in the 1930s.

Key

① Reeds

② Trumpets

③ Trombones

④ Rhythm

⑤ Strings

One of the early leaders of the Swing Band development was **Benny Goodman**, whose band first presented a 'hot' swinging style as part of their regular dance programme in 1934. By 1939 hundreds of Swing Bands were to be found, led by names like **Tommy Dorsey, Jimmy Dorsey, Gene Krupa,** and many more. Swing music developed alongside radio which, in 1934, was still something of a novelty. Radio stations in the USA would present two or three hours of swing music in an evening, divided up into 15-minute segments for different bands. Teenagers supported their own favourite band with the same excitement and enthusiasm as teenagers in the 1960s. Membership of bands fluctuated – the line-up changed frequently, with many players leaving bands to become band-leaders in their own right and others moving from band to band to play more jazz or more dance music, according to their taste.

'The Silent Dance' (1928) – A great loop of wire connected to an amplifier beneath the floor which in turn ran to a gramophone in the adjoining room. The dancers picked up the music by induction from the buried loop.

Perhaps the best of all Swing Bands were those led by **Duke Ellington** and **Count Basie**, and they often had the best jazz players in their bands. The Swing Band era reached its end with the end of World War Two and there are a number of reasons why its popularity declined at this time. In the USA a 20 per cent entertainment tax had been levied; television had begun to keep people at home; small groups were cheaper to hire than Big Bands. Jazz fans alone weren't enough to keep Big Bands going and other fans were simply looking for something new. But Big Bands never completely died out – many of the old band-leaders kept their bands going into the 1950s, '60s, and '70s and some into the 1980s!

The Swing Band era will always be remembered for bringing jazz into the mainstream of culture. For 20 to 30 years, jazz became the 'pop' music of the day. If you went to a dance, or put money into a juke box, or turned on the radio – sorry, wireless! – you would hear a Swing Band.

Find the band-leaders
- Count Basie
- Duke Ellington
- Benny Goodman
- Buddy Rich
- Stan Kenton
- Louis Armstrong
- Tommy Dorsey
- Bix Beiderbecke
- Glenn Miller
- Gene Krupa
- Paul Whiteman

O	N	P	Z	B	A	N	B	T	C	L	E	A	T	E	L	O	G
Z	O	A	G	L	E	B	E	N	N	Y	G	O	O	D	M	A	N
O	T	U	E	S	B	F	F	T	O	V	L	M	M	V	D	R	O
U	N	L	N	O	I	L	I	O	T	Z	E	B	M	W	C	Y	R
N	E	W	E	T	X	U	X	S	G	U	N	V	Y	L	V	S	T
D	K	H	K	U	B	Y	O	S	N	X	N	S	D	I	R	Z	S
U	N	I	R	N	E	A	A	C	I	K	M	J	O	D	J	L	M
M	A	T	U	N	I	X	S	I	L	C	I	P	R	C	E	S	R
T	T	E	P	O	D	C	U	I	L	K	L	T	S	F	V	L	A
E	S	M	A	D	E	Q	B	U	E	Q	L	S	E	M	A	H	S
E	A	A	E	C	R	M	S	R	E	U	E	M	Y	H	J	S	I
P	K	N	M	I	B	K	C	H	K	K	R	T	X	W	G	I	U
S	N	X	R	U	E	V	B	I	U	M	P	V	A	L	I	P	O
H	L	Z	J	O	C	B	U	D	D	Y	R	I	C	H	U	E	L
O	M	A	N	B	K	R	U	I	M	C	C	K	N	U	O	P	C
R	T	Y	F	S	E	O	B	O	A	U	W	B	K	A	N	R	W
N	M	S	K	N	E	T	N	J	P	R	H	V	L	D	E	L	X
Q	H	L	O	E	P	F	T	L	W	K	S	M	V	K	T	I	J

Buddy Rich, famous American band-leader and drummer, in England during his 1986 tour.

CAN YOU?

1 Listen to recordings of some Big Bands, and compare the Big Band sound with the backing used on some pop records and with some TV shows – what are the similarities?
2 Analyse the sound difference between, say, Glenn Miller and Benny Goodman, i.e. be as 'ear sensitive' as someone of your age might have been 40 or 50 years ago.
3 Write 8 bars of music for a full Big Band.

TALKING POINT

1 Many 'rehearsal-only' Big Bands survive today. Discuss with a group of friends why people still enjoy playing/making this type of music. What sort of problems would arise if one or two instrument players didn't turn up?
2 Is there a Big Band at your school – or at a school nearby? Do you play in it? Have you listened to it?
3 If you don't have a Big Band at school, do you have enough of the right instruments to create one?

Adding thirds

Adding thirds is one of those fairly simple but quite clever musical things that can OVERNIGHT transform an ordinary, dull tune into a Supertune! Well – No, nothing's that easy, but it's an interesting device to experiment and become familiar with. Glenn Miller did it a lot, so did the Everly Brothers.

There are four important things to understand first. (Refer to the chords section (page 48) if you want more help here.)

1 A chord is made up of a **root** – the lowest note, which gives the chord its name – a **third** (3rd) and a **fifth** (5th). If the tune is using the root you can add the third:

2 If the tune is using the third of the chord, you can add the fifth, which means that you've added a third above the third:

3 If you take a root and a third and turn it upside-down – putting the root over the top – you have added a **sixth** (6th) and this will sound as effective as adding a third:

4 You can add a third below as well as above!

So begin by playing or singing the following two tunes and then adding the thirds as shown. The chords are shown so that you, or someone, can put an accompaniment with the thirds.

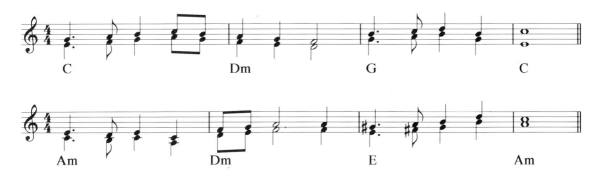

It takes a bit of confidence to do this straight off, so try to practise by 'singing along' with a record, tape or radio and don't worry if it doesn't always work; go further than a third if you need to – let your ear decide what is best. Have a go, then, with a friend – try some tunes you both know. 'Spanish Eyes' works well, so does 'Eleanor Rigby' by the **Beatles**.

The idea of adding thirds works equally well with
vocal and instrumental music – a third above or
below the given note or a sixth above or below.
Here's the opening to a 12-bar blues that works
nicely in thirds:

and with the added third:

Even **Beethoven** did it in this piece:

Some examples of adding sixths:

and with the added sixth:

Dm   G   C   Am

So try using this technique with some of your own
songs or blues or **reggae** numbers. It can be an
easy way of providing an interesting extra part.

Plastic discs and LP presentation

The 12-inch, 78 r.p.m. disc established itself as the standard disc on which recorded sound was presented, but it had many faults, chiefly: (a) its fragility, and (b) its limited playing time per side. Nevertheless, it remained an industry standard from the 1920s until the end of the 1940s. Many experiments were made with different diameters of disc, and different groove widths, but none proved wholly successful. It was not until the late 1940s that the first successful release of long-playing vinylite 33 r.p.m. **microgroove** discs was announced in America. There followed at the end of the 1940s a similar battle to that which had taken place some 40 years earlier between the phonograph and the gramophone. Different companies had found different ways of improving the old 78s' system and it made commercial sense for them to encourage the old system to continue. However, by 1955 the battle was decided and 78s were on the way out. The new **vinyl** discs were designed to play at 33 r.p.m., and were made in 10-inch, and 12-inch diameter sizes – the latter with a playing time of about 24 minutes per side. The new LPs (Long Players) were a great improvement on the old 78s, mainly in the reduction of surface noise – the hiss so familiar in 78 sound. The new records had a soft surface and required an extremely lightweight hard-tipped needle, now called a stylus. The 45 r.p.m. 7-inch record survived from the battle between companies, and with its playing time of around 4 minutes per side was ideal for the lighter side of the repertoire.

The first LP to achieve 1 million sales was the 1949 original-cast recording of **Rodgers' and Hammerstein's** *Oklahoma*! This had sold 15 million copies by 1958.

LP PRESENTATION

As 78s were quite heavy, they required robust cardboard sleeves which were difficult to print on. However, the new lightweight LPs gave record companies an opportunity to make a feature of sleeve designs and present detailed information about the recording, music, and artistes. From America came the idea of the 'browserie' – a selection of LP covers in boxes which allowed customers to be influenced by the cover design as well as their desire to hear a particular piece of music.

The LP of the original cast recording of *Oklahoma!* was the first to achieve 1 million sales.

CAN YOU?

1 Find any really old LPs (12-inch or 10-inch) and **EPs** (Extended Play – 7-inch, 33 r.p.m.) at home, at relatives, or at school.
2 Think of ways in which records are sold today – No! not just in the shops!
3 Write an original sleeve note for your favourite LP.
4 Make a list of items that would go on your ideal LP, saying who the songs are by and why you are including them.
5 Design a record sleeve, showing you and a group of friends as the stars.

TALKING POINT

1 Are there any record collectors in your class, or amongst parents, friends, etc? What kind of collections do they have, and why?
2 How much does the design of a record sleeve influence you when buying a record?
3 Does the video influence you when choosing records to buy?

Play jazz on your . . .

You can, of course, play in a jazz style on almost any instrument – a quick look at the next section will show you most of the possibilities. Playing jazz is difficult, although all the people who do it well make it look very easy. The answer is to do it! – even if you play lots of notes that don't sound right. It's a bit like riding a bike – you've got to fall off and scrape your knees a few times, and no amount of explanation will help to avoid that.

Here are some ideas – first of all for treble clef instruments, and then bass clef instruments. Remember to use this section in conjunction with *Improvisation* (pages 12–13), and *Jazzing a Tune* (pages 56–7).

FLUTE AND OBOE

Both have been used in jazz ensembles but have not earned regular places – perhaps because their tone quality doesn't allow them to compete easily with instruments like the trumpet, saxophone, etc. However, there's nothing to stop you playing music in a jazz style on your flute, or oboe, but it is important to play in a style that is suited to that particular instrument. Remember to use the best-sounding part of the range. For example, the following phrase is fine on a clarinet but much less effective on a flute because the flute lacks power in this register.

But here is a good flute example:

and an oboe one:

VIOLIN AND VIOLA

The violin gradually disappeared from its role as a front-line instrument (as it was used in the 1910s and 1920s), probably because its sound could not easily compete with the clarinet, saxophone, trumpet, trombone, etc., and in those early days of sound amplification it was not really practical to **'mike-up'** a violin. Several outstanding jazz violinists have maintained a jazz tradition on this instrument, exploiting its true versatility. The viola is a rarity in the jazz world, but there's no reason why you shouldn't try it – who knows, this could be the start of something quite enormous!

TROMBONE

One of the vital parts of the traditional band and used in 'trombone family' context in Big Bands and beyond. It's important to remember that the 'tenor' trombone is a **tenor** instrument, and is at its most effective in that range; too often it takes the place of a **bass** instrument and although capable of fulfilling this role, has to be carefully played to do this effectively.

BASSOON

Again, rarely a solo instrument because of its tone quality. However, if carefully 'miked up' there's no reason why it shouldn't be used. Play from trombone, or double-bass parts.

CLARINET AND SAXOPHONE

These instruments are ideally suited for jazz and you should listen to as many recorded or live performances as you can – it's one of the best ways to learn. Certain characteristics enable the clarinet and saxophone to play figures like these, which are ideal in jazz:

TRUMPET

Again, ideal for jazz – listen to as many examples as you can. The trumpet is as versatile as the clarinet and saxophone and can be used for all jazz styles. Here's a typical trumpet phrase:

CELLO

Somewhat of a rarity, like the bassoon and the viola, but certainly usable. Read trombone or double-bass parts.

DOUBLE-BASS

The great stand-by of the rhythm section because even when it's played incredibly badly with lots of wrong notes it adds an immediately helpful sound quality.

Slowly-in a smoky mood

Standard intro

Skiffle and rock 'n'roll

The City Ramblers were a popular skiffle group during the mid-1950s.

The end of the Second World War (1939–1945) marked the decline of the Swing/Big Band era, and it seems that musical fashion changed almost completely during the next few years – strongly influenced by financial considerations. It changed from the uneconomic, professional, full sound of the Swing Band to the home-made sound of **skiffle**.

The word 'skiffle' was originally used in the 1920s to describe a sort of jazz in which 'normal' instruments were replaced by 'home-made' ones. It was now used to describe a short, folk-music session during an evening devoted to jazz, and within a short time had developed into an independent musical form. The lyrics of skiffle were drawn from folk-blues from Black America.

Instrumentation included **kazoos**, **washboards**, **tea-chest**/broom handle **basses**, like the ones in the photograph above. By the way, you may not be familiar with a washboard – it was used to scrub clothes on, in the days before automatic washing machines.

It's difficult for us to understand why skiffle made such an impact, but this was partly because of its 'anyone-can-do-it' style, and its simple musical material. It was also due in no small part to the personality of its stars like **Lonnie Donegan**, and later, **Tommy Steele**. Oh sorry, if you're still wondering about the washboard, it was played by a person wearing thimbles – yes, honestly – find someone old enough and ask them!

The 1950s also marks the rise in popularity of the guitar, shown by this advertisement from a 1958 copy of *Exchange & Mart*. Skiffle contests were frequently promoted in cinemas and theatres, often replacing the usual Saturday matinée, with winners being decided by the quantity and quality of applause.

While skiffle was all the rage in Britain, an important development in popular music in the USA at this time was that of **rock 'n' roll**. Rock 'n' roll used the 12-bar blues chord pattern from jazz, but now played 'up-tempo' with electric guitar and a lead singer. It appealed to teenagers because it was different; it was rebellious – and it was their own music – in just the same way that Swing music had appealed to teenagers in the 1930s. Two of the great stars were **Elvis Presley** and **Buddy Holly** and the group **Bill Haley and the Comets**. 'Real' rock 'n' roll only surfaced in a small way and for a short time – there were too many other styles on the market for listeners to choose from, and many preferred the more 'respectable' styles of Swing or small-group Swing or the respectability offered by the **Everly Brothers** from America. At the end of the 1950s that respectability was provided in England by **Cliff Richard**.

CAN YOU?

1 Listen to a recording of some skiffle music – Lonnie Donegan's 'Rock Island Line' is a good example if you can get hold of it. Then put a skiffle group together and play some skiffle.
2 Listen to some rock 'n' roll and write a rock song in late-1950s' style.
3 Interview a parent or friend about the 1950s. Ask them if they remember how they felt then. What sort of dances did they do to skiffle and rock 'n' roll?
4 Do you know anyone who dresses as a **teddy boy**? Talk to him and find out how much he knows about the teddy-boys of the 1950s.
5 Make a tea-chest bass; or find a washboard in a junk shop and try playing it – do the thimbles help?!
6 Draw a washboard and a tea-chest bass. Can you think of, design and draw any other instruments like this that will be cheap and easy to make and simple to play?

TALKING POINT

1 Why does the 'rebellious teenager' idea keep coming round?
2 Can you think of reasons why rock 'n' roll became popular after the Second World War – what did young people think and feel in Britain?
3 Why didn't skiffle and rock 'n' roll last longer than they did? Do you think that rock 'n' roll will come back again as so many other styles have?
4 Does any other musical style use such ordinary instruments as skiffle? Think about music in other countries.
5 How does the age of rock 'n' roll singers of the 1950s compare with pop singers' ages today?
6 Imagine wearing your hair like this!

Stars of the Fifties (clockwise from left):
Elvis Presley; Tommy Steele; Cliff Richard; Jiving to Cy
Laurie's Jazz Band; Everly Brothers; Bill Haley and the
Comets; Buddy Holly; Connie Francis.

The 12-bar blues (2)

It helps to work through *The 12-Bar Blues (1)* first.
This section presents a slightly more complicated
blues for you to sing and play and includes sections
which you can improvise in and generally add
things to. You should find *Riffs and Easy Figures*
helpful and use the Index (back) and Contents
(front) to help find other sections.

This blues is similar to those played in the mid-
1950s at the time when rock 'n' roll was surfacing
in Great Britain – growing out of the skiffle boom
(see pages 30–31).

Remember to end on the chord of C
when you play the final repeat.

Piano

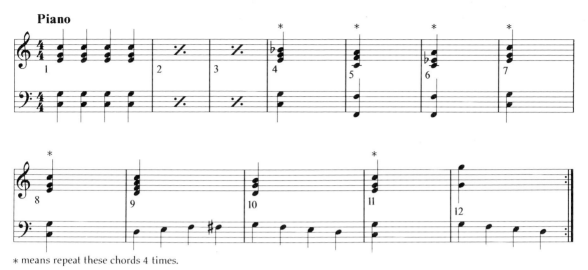

* means repeat these chords 4 times.

Easy bass

Play the name note of the chord.

Easy glock

ROCK RHYTHMS

Use these rhythms with this 12-bar blues. Practise saying them first, then play them on the instruments.

Keep repeating this two-bar pattern.

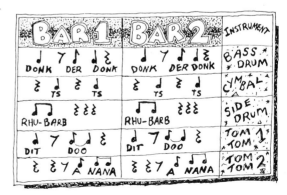

The 12-bar blues (3) - jazz

This is the most difficult of the blues to play and sing. You may find it helpful to work through *The 12-Bar Blues (1)* and *(2)* first, but it's not essential.

This form of the blues involves more complicated chords, but if you take it gently you should manage it. First of all, the basic chord pattern:

(See page 34.)

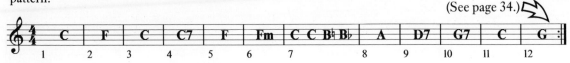

Although this blues is more difficult, it should work well and give you a good backing over which to improvise your own tunes.

If you compare this with *The 12-Bar Blues (1)* and *(2)*, you'll see that there are many similarities. You can also probably work out that the troublesome bar is bar 7, but this and the final few bars give this version its characteristic 'jazz' flavour.

THE TUNE

Make up your own! Improvise it; busk it – if all else fails just play the top line of the piano part, but you should be able to do better than that!

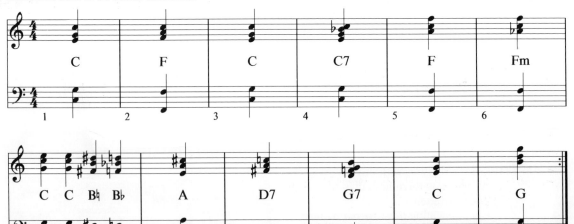

You can easily put a **walking bass** into the last few bars of this blues and it will be particularly effective. There are several ways of doing it – here's one to try:

Below are some easy instrumental parts – add as many as you can.

And some rhythm parts that you can add to make it sound more complete:

Glossary

ABBA: A Swedish pop group with four members whose first hit was 'Waterloo', released in 1974.

ACCENT: A symbol above or below a note which tells you to stress this note more than the others.

ACOUSTIC: An acoustic guitar is one which does not use an amplifier. We talk about the acoustic properties of a building when describing how things sound there.

AMPLIFIER: A piece of electronic equipment which magnifies an electronic signal.

ANT, Adam: A 1980s' pop singer who made great use of video in his sales promotion.

ARMSTRONG, Louis: 1900–71. An American jazz singer and trumpeter whose career spanned the early New Orleans days of traditional jazz through to television variety shows in the 1960s.

AUGMENTED: Literally means 'made bigger'. An augmented chord means that the fifth of the chord is sharpened.

BANANARAMA: British all-female group with successes dating from the early 1980s.

BARS: Music is commonly divided into bars, each containing the same number of beats.

BASIE, Count: 1904–84. An American pianist and Big Band leader.

BASS: The lowest-sounding male voice; also applies to instruments like the bassoon and double-bass, which of course read from the bass clef.

BBC: British Broadcasting Corporation, which was founded in 1927, and exercises a strong influence on the listening taste of the public.

BEATLES: Perhaps the most famous pop group of the 1960s – Paul McCartney, John Lennon, George Harrison and Ringo Starr.

BEETHOVEN, Ludwig van: 1770–1827. A German composer whose life spans the period of change between Classicism and Romanticism.

BEIDERBECKE, Bix: 1903–30. A German-American cornet player.

BENSON ORCHESTRA OF CHICAGO: Another famous 1920s band, who experimented with recording techniques.

BIG BAND: The name given to an instrumental combination of 5 saxophones, 5 trumpets, 4 trombones, and rhythm section, that was popular in the 1930s.

BLUE NOTES: Characteristic notes of blues singers or players which approximate to the flattened third, fifth and seventh of the diatonic scale.

BLUES: The foundation of jazz, blues songs were work songs from the southern states of northern America sung by slaves shipped over from Africa. As they were forbidden to speak in their own languages while working, they sang to communicate with each other and to ease the monotony of their work.

BOLAN, Marc: A British pop star of the early 1970s.

BOSSA NOVA: A characteristic Latin-American rhythm.

BOWIE, David: A British pop star who has had chart successes regularly since 1969.

BOY GEORGE: A mid-1980s transvestite pop star.

BROOKS, Elkie: A female British pop singer who has had chart successes since 1977.

CABASA: A Latin-American percussion instrument.

CAKEWALK: A Black American dance from the 1880s which involved slaves performing a strutting dance in parody of their white masters.

CALIFORNIA RAMBLERS: Another band of the 1920s, they were in competition with Paul Whiteman. Famous for titles such as 'Vo-Do-De-O Blues'.

CAPO: A device placed around the neck of a guitar which presses all the strings against the fingerboard, thus allowing the player to easily play in a different key.

CASSETTE: The compact cassette was introduced in 1964.

CASSIDY, David: A British pop star whose chart successes were in the early 1970s, after which he moved into musicals.

CASTLE, Irene and Vernon: Professional dancing couple famous in the 1910–20 era for demonstrating dance steps.

CHORD: A group of two of more notes played or sung at the same time.

CHORD SYMBOLS/SIGNS: Two shorthand methods of writing down chords without using music manuscript paper.

CHORUS: The most memorable part of a song; or a group of singers.

CLAPTON, Eric: Lead guitar with the Yardbirds and Cream, whose hits have continued into the 1980s.

CLASSICAL: A word wrongly used by many people when referring to music of which they are not particularly fond. The Classical era extended roughly from about 1750 to 1800.

CLEF: The sign placed at the beginning of a stave to indicate which lines and spaces are being used for which notes.

COMBO: A combination of players, or an amplifier and loudspeaker housed in one container.

COMPACT DISC: The most modern readily affordable means of storing sound information that can be easily reproduced when required.

COON-SANDERS NIGHT-HAWKS: Dance band of the 1920s who always made interesting recordings with their drummer and leader, Carleton Coon.

CREOLE, KID and the COCOANUTS: An American female vocal group with a male singer.

CROTCHET: A one-beat note.

DAMNED, The: A late-1970s' Punk group.

DÉPÊCHE MODE: A 1980s' group from the UK with many chart successes.

DIATONIC: The name given to the major and minor scales.

DIGITAL: Recording system which stores information in a more efficient manner than the 'analogue' system.

DIMINISHED: Literally means made smaller and is used to describe musical intervals that are one semitone smaller than minor. A dim. chord is made up of minor thirds, but so named because of its diminished fifth.

DOLBY: Raymond Dolby is the inventor of the now universally accepted system of noise reduction on compact cassette players.

DONEGAN, Lonnie: A leading exponent of Skiffle in the 1950s.

DORSEY, Tommy and Jimmy: American musicians whose fame grew during the Big Band era.

DOUBLING: A person who plays more than one instrument is a doubler. It is usual for clarinet players to double on saxophone, for example.

DRUM: There are many different kinds of drum. The word drum is often associated with kit.

DURAN DURAN: A British group from the 1980s with many chart successes

DURATION: When applied to music, how long a sound lasts.

DVOŘÁK, Antonin: 1841–1904. Czech composer who wrote the New World Symphony following a visit to the USA.

DYLAN, Bob: A singer associated with protest songs who first became famous in 1965 with 'Times they are a-changin''.

DYNAMIC: A term used in connection with louds and softs in music.

ECHO and the BUNNYMEN: A British group from the 1980s.

ELECTRIC LIGHT ORCHESTRA: A British vocal and instrumental group with chart successes from 1972 onwards.

ELGAR, Sir Edward: 1857–1934. English composer famous for writing 'Land of Hope and Glory'.

ELLINGTON, Duke: 1899–1974. American composer, pianist and bandleader who achieved international recognition.

ELLIS, Don: 1934–78. American jazz musician and composer who became interested in Indian music and used complex rhythm patterns in his compositions.

EP: Extended Play. Refers to a record that is 7 inches across but can play for about 12 minutes per side.

ESSEX, David: A British vocalist who has been in the charts since 1973.

EUROPE, James: American bandleader popular in Europe in the 1910s.

EVERLY BROTHERS: An American male vocal duo who had their first success in 1957 and were again in the charts in 1984.

FAITH, Adam: One of the pop stars whose career spanned the period of change between the end of the 1950s and the emergence of Merseyside groups in the early 1960s.

FIFTH: The fifth note of a scale.

FISHWALK: A dance style that came before the foxtrot.

FLAT: A sign placed before a note that lowers that note by one semitone.

FLOWER POWER: A short-lived pop movement of the late 1960s.

FORM: We speak of musical form meaning the pattern that a piece follows.

FOXTROT: A dance, still popular today, that was created around 1910.

FREDDY and the DREAMERS: A group from Merseyside that was popular in the 1960s.

GARFUNKEL, SIMON and: A popular American singing duo that came together in the 1960s.

GERRY and the PACEMAKERS: A 1960s' Merseyside group.

GERSHWIN, George: 1889–1937. American composer and pianist, whose *Rhapsody in Blue* for piano and orchestra and *Porgy and Bess*, an opera, are still widely performed and popular.

GLITTER, Gary: A British singer popular since the early 1970s.

GLOCKENSPIEL: A tuned percussion instrument with metal bars that are hit with beaters.

GOLDKETTE, Jean: A bandleader and organizer of bands famous in the 1920s, who employed many famous jazz musicians.

GOODMAN, Benny: 1909–86. American band-leader and clarinettist famous in the Swing era and popular since.

GORDY, Berry: The founder of Motown.

GRACE NOTE: Ornamental or decorative note, usually played lightly and quickly before the main note.

GRAMOPHONE: Early sound machine that played discs rather than cylinders.

GRAND: The large sort of non-upright piano.

GUTHRIE, Woody: 1912–67. American urban folk singer from the post-Second World War early days of modern 'popular' music.

HALEY, Bill and the COMETS: 1950s' Rock 'n' roll group who made 'Rock around the Clock' famous in 1955.

HARMONIC: Ask your physics teacher; but briefly it's one of the components of what you hear as a single sound. It's also one form of the minor scale.

HARMONICA: Sometimes called a mouth organ.

HARMONIUM: A keyboard instrument in which the sound is produced by blowing air through reeds. The air comes from bellows which are operated by the player's feet.

HARMONY: An effective combination of notes produces harmony.

HARPSICHORD: A keyboard instrument in which the sound is produced by the strings being plucked.

HEIFETZ, Jascha: A famous, Russian-born, US violinist.

HENDRIX, Jimi: 1947–70. Famous rock guitarist whose Anglo-American group the Jimi Hendrix Experience had hits in the early 1970s.

HOLLY, Buddy: 1936–1959. An American vocalist whose hits at the end of the 1950s secured him fame for many years to follow.

HOOK: The bit of a song that you remember, or in other words the bit of a song that sells it.

HORSETROT: A dance that was popular at the time of the foxtrot's first appearance.

IMPROVISATION: Making it up as you go along.

IPANA TROUBADOURS: A band sponsored by Ipana toothpaste in the 1920s.

JACKSONS: An American family group that had hits from the 1970s onwards.

JAZZ: Music in which improvisation is an essential ingredient.

JINGLE: Short piece of music used in an advertisement.

JOHN, Elton: British pop star with hits dating back to 1970.

JOPLIN, Janis: A rock 'n' roll singer who was an early victim of the late-1960s drug scene.

KAZOO: A home-made musical instrument based on the bigophone, an instrument credited to Frenchman Jacques Bigot.

KENTON, Stan: 1912–79. American pianist and band-leader who rose to fame during the Big Band era.

KEY: The concept of key developed in the sixteenth century with the development of equal temperament.

KEY SIGNATURE: The sharps or flats written at the beginning of each line of music to indicate the key of the piece.

KEYBOARDS: A term now used to describe any instrument with piano-like keys.

KINKS: A 1960s' British group who have reappeared in the 1980s.

KRUPA, Gene: 1909–73. American drummer who played with and led many famous bands.

LANG, Eddie: 1902–33. American guitarist who, despite his short life, gained great recognition for his talent.

LATIN-AMERICAN: Term applied to denote particular rhythmic influences.

LEGER: Short lines which enable notes to be placed above or below the stave.

LENNON, John: 1940–80. One of the Beatles.

LP: Long Playing. A term used to distinguish microgroove 12-inch records from 78s.

LSD: Widely used hallucinatory drug in the 1960s.

LULLABY of BIRDLAND: Tune composed by George Shearing which has become a standard.

MAJOR: Term used to describe keys, scales, and intervals as well as chords.

MARACAS: Latin-American percussion instrument which in its original form consisted of a dried gourd filled with seeds.

MARLEY, Bob: 1945–81. A Jamaican reggae vocalist and guitarist who, with his group the Wailers, was successful in the late 1970s.

MELANIE: American female vocalist whose song 'Brand new key' brought her success in 1972.

MELODIC: Term used to denote one form of the minor scale.

MERSEYSIDE: The banks of the River Mersey at Liverpool, which refers to the fact that many 1960s' groups came from there.

METALLOPHONE: Tuned percussion instrument with metal bars.

MICROGROOVE: The sort of grooves found on a long-playing record.

MICROPHONE: An electronic device which converts sounds into electrical signals.

MIDDLE EIGHT: The middle eight bars of a song that people find difficult to remember.

MIKED-UP: Refers to the amplifying of a voice or instrument.

MILLER, Glenn: 1904–44. American trombonist, arranger and composer whose fame is now legendary.

MINIM: A two-beat note.

MINOR: Term used to describe keys, scales, intervals and chords.

MINSTREL SHOWS: Consisted of white singers and musicians who dressed up as negroes and performed music inspired by the early Negro folk music. They were very popular throughout America in the early part of this century.

MONKEES: Anglo-American group created in the late 1960s to rival the Beatles.

MOODY BLUES: British group with chart successes dating back to 1964.

MOTOWN: Literally motor town, i.e. Detroit in the USA, where cars are manufactured. The term refers to the many successful artistes schooled by Berry Gordy.

NATURAL: A note which is not a sharp or a flat, and the name of a sign placed before a note which cancels a previous sharp or flat.

NEW WAVE: The fashions etc. associated with the rise of Punk in the late 1970s.

NEWTON-JOHN, Olivia: British vocalist with many successes since the early 1970s.

ORGAN (Church): An instrument with a long history. The sound is produced by blowing air through reeds and pipes.

ORGAN: (Electric): the modern equivalent of the church organ.

OSMONDS: A talented American musical family who have made many hit records.

OSTINATO: Term applied to a repeated pattern in music.

PARTON, Dolly: American country and western singer.

PASSING NOTES: Technical term used in the study of harmony and best explained by your teacher and/or harmony book.

PIANO: Short for pianoforte which, when translated from the Italian, means soft-loud.

PITCH: The relative highness or lowness of a note.

PITCH PIPES: Used to check tuning on a stringed instrument like the guitar or violin.

POLICE: Anglo-American group with many chart successes.

POP: Short for popular.

PRACTICE COMBO: A small amplifier and loudspeaker combined that produces a relatively low volume.

PRESLEY, Elvis: 1935–77. American vocalist and guitarist who led Rock 'n' roll from 1956.

PUNK: A trend in pop in the late 1970s.

QUATRO, Suzi: American vocalist with many hits in the 1970s.

QUAVER: A note worth half a beat.

RAGTIME: Term used to describe a style of piano playing and composition popular towards the end of the last century.

REGGAE: West Indian style of music with a strong, syncopated beat.

REST: A sign which indicates silence in a bar of music.

RHYTHM SECTION: Usually refers to part of a Big Band, consisting of piano, bass, drums, and guitar.

RICH, Buddy: 1917–87. American band-leader and drummer who continued successfully from the 1940s.

RICHARD, Cliff: Everlasting British pop star with hits dating back to 1958.

RIFFS: Short repeated figures in jazz.

ROCK 'n' ROLL: A trend in popular music which emerged in the mid-1950s.

RODGERS and HAMMER-STEIN: Composer and lyricist of many famous musicals.

ROLLING STONES: Famous group of the 1960s who rivalled the Beatles.

ROOT: Technical term describing the key note of a chord.

ROSS, Diana: One of the most successful of Motown stars who first appeared with the Supremes.

ROUND THE FIFTHS: A progression from tonic→dominant→tonic, i.e. C—G—D— etc. which allows a composer to build up a sequence easily and make an easy modulation.

ROXY MUSIC: British group that has been successful since the early 1970s.

SAN FRANCISCO: City on the west coast of North America which is and has been an important centre in music.

SCABIES, Rat: Drummer with The Damned, a 1970s Punk group.

SCALE: Pattern of notes that is memorable and can be transposed.

SEGOVIA, Andrés: 1894–1987. Spanish guitarist who made classical guitar playing a respected art form in the twentieth century.

SEMIBREVE: A note worth four beats.

SEMIQUAVER: A note worth quarter of a beat.

SEMITONE: The smallest easily measurable gap or interval between sounds.

SEVENTH: A chord consisting of the root, third, fifth and seventh in the scale.

SEX PISTOLS: 1970s' British punk group.

SHADOWS: British instrumental and vocal group of long-standing fame.

SHARP: A sign which, when placed before a note, raises that note by one semitone.

SHEARING, George: Blind English composer and pianist who works in the jazz idiom.

SIMON and GARFUNKEL: American singing duo who were most successful in the 1960s.

SIMON, Carly: American female singer with hits in the early 1970s.

SIXTH: The sixth note of a scale.

SKIFFLE: The flowering of home-made music-making in the mid-1950s.

SLADE: British group with successes dating back to 1971.

SOUL: As much a way of presentation as of style in music but nevertheless clearly identifiable.

SOUL, David: Mid-1970s' American vocalist famous also for his TV series.

STANDARD: A tune that has become widely accepted, probably outside the audience for which it was originally intended.

STAVE: The set of 5 lines on which music is written.

STEELE, Tommy: British singer whose hits came between 1956 and 1961. He has since become a highly successful entertainer and starred in musicals.

STEWART, Rod: British vocalist with many successes.

STRAIGHT: Not jazz, or pop, and not played in Swing style.

STRAVINSKY, Igor: 1882–1971. Russian composer particularly famous for his ballet music.

STRUM: The stroking of the strings of, say, a guitar, with the hand.

SUPREMES: Motown group of the 1960s.

SUS CHORD: A chord without a third. Instead it has a fourth which just can't wait to become a third. It was a common sound in the 1960s.

SWEET: British group of the 1970s.

SWING: The opposite of straight when speaking of playing styles.

SYNCOPATION: Music with strongly accented off-beats.

SYNTHESIZER: Electronic instrument which changes given sounds.

TEA-CHEST BASS: Home-made 'double bass' which was popular in the Skiffle era.

TEDDY BOY: Characteristically dressed person dating back to the 1950s.

TENOR: The higher of the two common male voices; also used to describe instruments in this range.

TIN-PAN ALLEY: The world of publishing and promotions associated with popular music.

TONIC: The root, or key note of a scale.

TRADITIONAL JAZZ: As distinct from modern, etc.

TRANSPOSITION: Changing pitch without loss of melodic identity.

TREBLE: Relatively high pitched.

TWIGGY: Very thin female British model and singer from the mid-1970s.

UNDERGROUND: Styles in popular music that appeal to a limited market.

UPRIGHT: The smaller and more common sort of piano.

VERSE: The part of a song that people often can't remember.

VINYL: Sort of plastic that records are made from.

WALKING BASS: Bass line that moves at a speed of one note per beat.

WARING, Fred: Led a very popular dance band in the 1920s and continued to work in popular music since, concentrating more on choirs and vocalists.

WASHBOARD: Domestic appliance use as a percussion instrument in the mid 1950s.

WHAM: Successful 1980s' British group.

WHITEMAN, Paul: 1890–1957. American violinist and bandleader known as the 'king of jazz' who was highly successful in the 1920s.

WHO, The: British group from the 1960s.

WILLIAMS, John: Guitarist who has successfully worked in both classical and pop fields.

WONDER, Stevie: Blind American pianist, harmonica player, and composer of Motown originals.

WYNETTE, Tammy: American country and western singer.

Rudiments

Use this section of the book for reference – it might help to explain things when you get stuck.

When music is written down we have to show two important things:

1 How long the sound lasts = **duration**
2 How high or low the note is = **pitch**

There are different ways of doing this, but the Western world uses the methods shown below.

DURATION

Sounds are written down as NOTES. Each note is said to last for a number of BEATS, or part of one beat. Each sort of note has a special name.

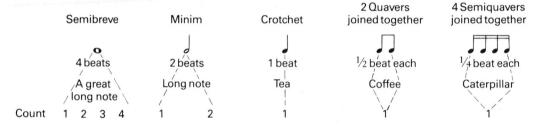

	Semibreve	Minim	Crotchet	2 Quavers joined together	4 Semiquavers joined together
	4 beats	2 beats	1 beat	½ beat each	¼ beat each
	A great long note	Long note	Tea	Coffee	Caterpillar
Count	1 2 3 4	1 2	1	1	1

Of course, it's very difficult to count semiquavers (¼ beats) individually, so clap a steady beat and say:

Tea	(Crotchet)	1 beat or clap
Coffee	(Quavers)	½ beat or 2 notes per clap
Long note	(Minim)	2 beats or claps
A great long note	(Semibreve)	4 beats or claps
Caterpillar	(Semiquavers)	¼ beat each or 4 notes per clap

For minims and semibreves you count the beats in your head. It's up to you or the composer what speed the beats go.

By the way, the Americans use a slightly different system – they call a ♩ a quarter note; a 𝅗𝅥 a half note, and so on.

RESTS

When writing down music it's very important to be able to show silences – **rests** – when you need them. So, here are the rests to match up with the notes shown in this section:

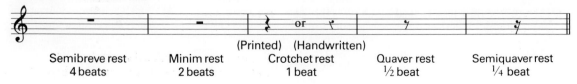

		(Printed) (Handwritten)		
Semibreve rest	Minim rest	Crotchet rest	Quaver rest	Semiquaver rest
4 beats	2 beats	1 beat	½ beat	¼ beat

REPEATS

All composers use musical shorthand to save time and there are three ways of indicating that music should be played again:

1 A set of two dots – the ordinary repeat sign, which means go back to the beginning and play it again, or go back to the last set of two dots:

2 The direct repeat sign telling you to play one or two bars again:

3 First and second time bars. It takes a lot of words to explain but if you follow the bar numbers in the next example you should be able to understand. Remember if there's anything that you are not sure about, ask your teacher.

PITCH

We use sets of five lines called **staves**. Notes are written 'on' the lines or 'between' the lines. A **clef** sign is put at the beginning of each stave.

It is generally thought easier to read notes that are on the stave than above it or below it, so different clefs are used to help.

The commonest are the **treble** clef:

and the **bass** clef:

Middle C

Middle C is shown here on the four commonest clefs:

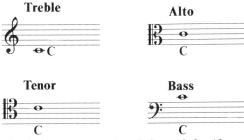

(But let's not get emotional about clefs – if you really want to know, your teacher will help you.)

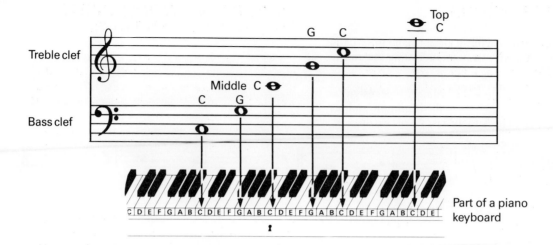

Part of a piano keyboard

The diagram above represents the middle section of a **piano** keyboard and shows the position of those notes on the stave. Compare this with the next diagram – as you can see, there are 88 notes on most pianos and the staves don't have room for all of them, so higher or lower notes are fitted on using **leger** lines. These extend the range of the staves. Remember that Middle C is easy to find on the piano, because it's near the keyhole.

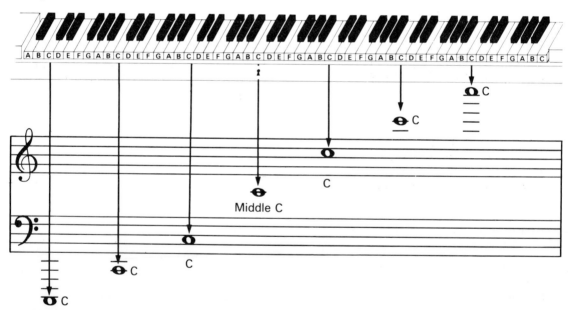

SHARPS AND FLATS

The white notes on the piano are all given names, as you can see from the piano diagrams. To refer to the black notes we talk of flats or sharps. It works like this: if two notes on the piano are next-door to each other they are said to be 1 **semitone** apart – this is the smallest measurable musical gap or interval. So, to go from F to G on the piano means to go up 2 semitones or 1 whole tone. The black note immediately to the right of F is F **sharp** (F♯) or G **flat** (G♭). The black note to the right of C is C sharp (C♯) or D flat (D♭). Just to confuse the issue the white note C can be referred to as B sharp! Think slowly about it and ask a friend to explain it as well – you'll soon get the hang of it.

By the way, we use a **natural** sign (♮) to cancel a sharp or flat.

SCALES AND KEYS

Since the early 1700s, music has been written in major or minor **keys**. Each key uses a **scale** of seven different notes, which are written on alternate lines and spaces. So C major scale uses the following notes:

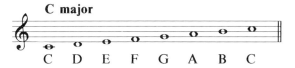

while D major needs F♯ and C♯ to produce a similarly corresponding pattern of notes:

The sharps or flats are shown as the **key signature** at the beginning of each line of music.

Minor keys share their key signatures with their relative major, which is situated three semitones below the key note of the major key. Minor scales exist in two forms – **harmonic** and **melodic**.

D major shares its key signature:

with B minor –

(a) the harmonic version:

(b) the melodic version:

MORE INFORMATION ABOUT MINOR SCALES AND KEYS

Composers don't write in the harmonic *or* the melodic form of the scale – they use a mixture of both, simply writing in a minor key. This is quite a difficult thing to do, so get as much help as you can from the book, and also ask your music teacher, and anyone who has passed their Grade 5 theory, because they should be able to help you as well.

KEY SIGNATURES

You may ask, 'Why not write everything in C major and avoid all the sharps and flats? It looks like it would be much easier.' Yes, there is some truth in that. However, the following points need to be thought about:

1 The key of C major may not suit a person's vocal range.

2 Guitarists prefer chords like E, A, D, G, etc., rather than C, and F.

3 Trumpet, saxophone, and clarinet players prefer B♭, E♭, etc., so you have to choose your key to fit best with the instruments and voices that you are writing for.

KEY SIGNATURES CHART

Here you can see the names of the major keys together with their relative minors. The numbers indicate the number of sharps or flats in the key signature.

When you write a key signature, the sharps or flats must always be written in a particular order.

The order for sharps is: F – C – G – D – A – E – B
and for flats is: B – E – A – D – G – C – F

TRANSPOSITION

This, unfortunately, is another thorny problem. Briefly, the word means changing to a higher, or lower pitch, and usually involves changing key, and key signature. You may be lucky enough to have an electronic keyboard which can do this for you, but for most people it will mean quite a lot of hard work, and writing out, so that other people can play it. A number of instruments are described as 'transposing instruments', for example the clarinet in Bb, tenor saxophone in Bb, etc., and this means that music for them must be written differently – look at the transposition chart.

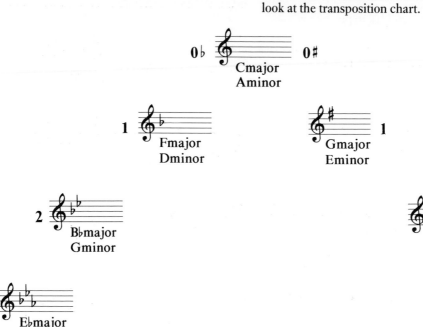

0♭ — C major / A minor — 0♯

1 — F major / D minor   G major / E minor — 1

2 — Bb major / G minor   D major / B minor — 2

3 — Eb major / C minor   A major / F♯ minor — 3

4 — Ab major / F minor   E major / C♯ minor — 4

5 — Db major / Bb minor   B major / G♯ minor — 5

6 — Gb major / Eb minor   F♯ major / D♯ minor — 6

TRANSPOSITION CHART

This chart deals with the more common transposing instruments. Flutes, oboes, violins and cellos are 'in C', i.e. they play the sound that they read. If you are uncertain, try to get someone to play a few notes for you – a practical instrumental demonstration will speak volumes, as will advice from the player concerned.

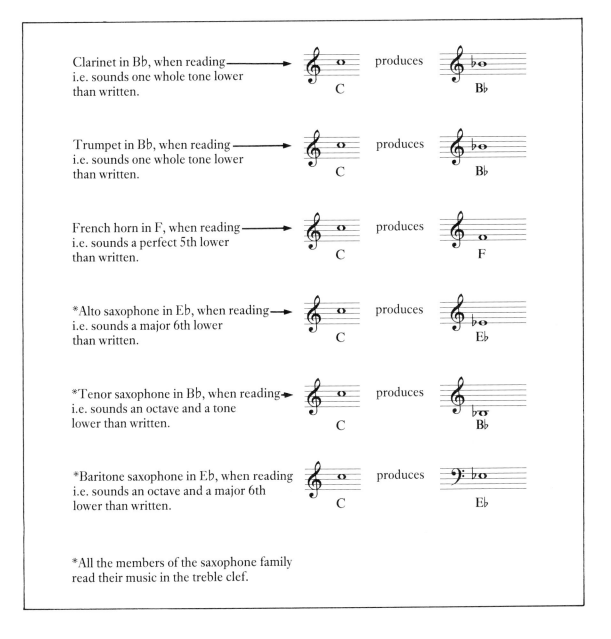

Clarinet in Bb, when reading i.e. sounds one whole tone lower than written.

C — produces — Bb

Trumpet in Bb, when reading i.e. sounds one whole tone lower than written.

C — produces — Bb

French horn in F, when reading i.e. sounds a perfect 5th lower than written.

C — produces — F

*Alto saxophone in Eb, when reading i.e. sounds a major 6th lower than written.

C — produces — Eb

*Tenor saxophone in Bb, when reading i.e. sounds an octave and a tone lower than written.

C — produces — Bb

*Baritone saxophone in Eb, when reading i.e. sounds an octave and a major 6th lower than written.

C — produces — Eb

*All the members of the saxophone family read their music in the treble clef.

47

Chords for pop and jazz

Some sections of the book, like this one for example, contain a lot of detailed information to help you with the practical work. You don't have to work through line by line – you can just 'dip in' for things that you need to know to help you play or compose a piece.

Most light music is made up of a tune and a 'backing' of chords – that is groups of notes played together. Most people can pick out a tune that they like on the piano or on a glock or recorder, but to make that tune sound like the original you need to understand chords.

Chord of F major   F G A B C

Chord of G major   Chord of A minor

*Simple chords have three notes in.
*The chord is named from the bottom note and is called Major or Minor.
*You build the chord by adding the next two notes on lines or in spaces.
*Major chords have 4 semitones between the bottom note and the middle note.
*Minor chords have 3 semitones between the bottom note and the middle note.

*♯ = a **sharp** sign – placed in front of a note it means that you must read or play that note one **semitone** higher.

*♭ = a **flat** sign – placed in front of a note it means that you must read or play that note one semitone lower.

*♮ = a **natural** sign – placed in front of a note cancels a previous sharp or flat.

*A **semitone** is a small difference in pitch between two notes. On the piano we say that two notes are a semitone apart if they are actually 'next-door' to each other – look at the diagram at the top of the page.

Here's a tune that most people can actually manage with its chords:

Try it on the piano with one or two of you on the tune and as many as you need on the chords.

CHOOSING THE RIGHT CHORD

This is difficult and needs experience but it's fun to see what happens. So, try this fairly well-known tune and use one of the chords underneath to find out which one you usually hear when the piece is played or sung. You can play the chords on glocks, guitars, piano, or electric keyboards.

Possible chords:	C	C	C	C		F	F	G
	F	F	G	G		Am	Am	C
	Am	Am	Em	Em		Dm	Dm	Em

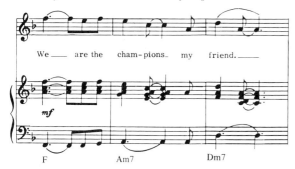

CHORD NAMES

Pop and jazz musicians use chords names like those just shown as a sort of shorthand to avoid having to write the notes down all the time. If you buy the sheet music for a popular song it will usually have all the notes written out as well as the chord names so that you can read whichever you prefer.

We ___ are the cham-pions_ my friend. ___

F   Am7   Dm7

MORE DIFFICULT CHORDS

The **seventh** chord
(a) On top of a minor chord add a flattened seventh (3 semitones up). (Your teacher will help.)

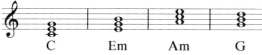

(b) On top of a major chord add an ordinary seventh or a flattened seventh.

The diminished chord
On top of any note, build up three more so that each note is 3 semitones away from its neighbour.

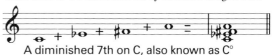

A diminished 7th on C, also known as C°

The sus chord
'Sus' is short for suspended, and this is a chord without a third. Instead, it has a fourth which just can't wait to become a third. It was a common sound in the 1960s.

G sus   G augmented

The augmented chord
Like the diminished chord but augmented means 'made bigger', and what happens is that the fifth of the chord is sharpened.

CHORD SOUNDS

Major – sounds 'firm', 'friendly', 'confident', 'stable' – no words can really describe a musical sound, but these might help you to recognize a major chord.

Minor – 'Firm' but 'sad'. Compare it with the major.

Seventh – Major third and flattened (minor) seventh:

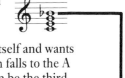

Richer than the major by itself and wants to move so that the seventh falls to the A in this case, which will then be the third of the new chord. So the new chord is:

Major seventh – A hard, modern-sounding chord used much in modern '70s' pop and jazz. It's now acceptable to end a piece on this chord although it's not a resting sound because the seventh always wants to move.

C△7 or Cmajor7   Dm7

Minor seventh – 'Sad' and 'soulful', it adds a smooth and full sound to any accompaniment.

INSTRUMENTS OF JAZZ

This page shows the four main sections of most jazz bands: REEDS, BRASS, RHYTHM, and STRINGS. Remember that a jazz band can be anything from 2 players, a duo, up to a full size jazz orchestra. A full string section is a rarity but there are many violinists who play jazz and, of course, the Double Bass is very important. Jazz players refer to the rhythm section and the "front line" – the people who play "the tune". Look out for a jazz band locally or on tele and see what the "line-up" is.

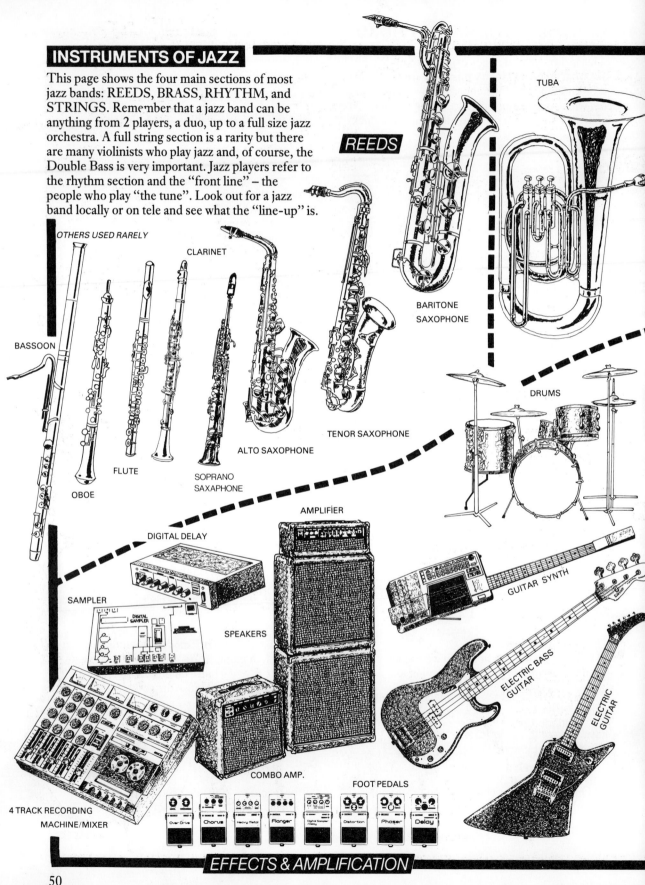

REEDS

TUBA

BARITONE SAXOPHONE

OTHERS USED RARELY

CLARINET

BASSOON

FLUTE

OBOE

SOPRANO SAXAPHONE

ALTO SAXOPHONE

TENOR SAXOPHONE

DRUMS

AMPLIFIER

DIGITAL DELAY

SAMPLER

SPEAKERS

GUITAR SYNTH

ELECTRIC BASS GUITAR

ELECTRIC GUITAR

COMBO AMP.

FOOT PEDALS

Over Drive Chorus Heavy Metal Flanger Digital Sampler/Delay Distortion Phaser Delay

4 TRACK RECORDING MACHINE/MIXER

EFFECTS & AMPLIFICATION

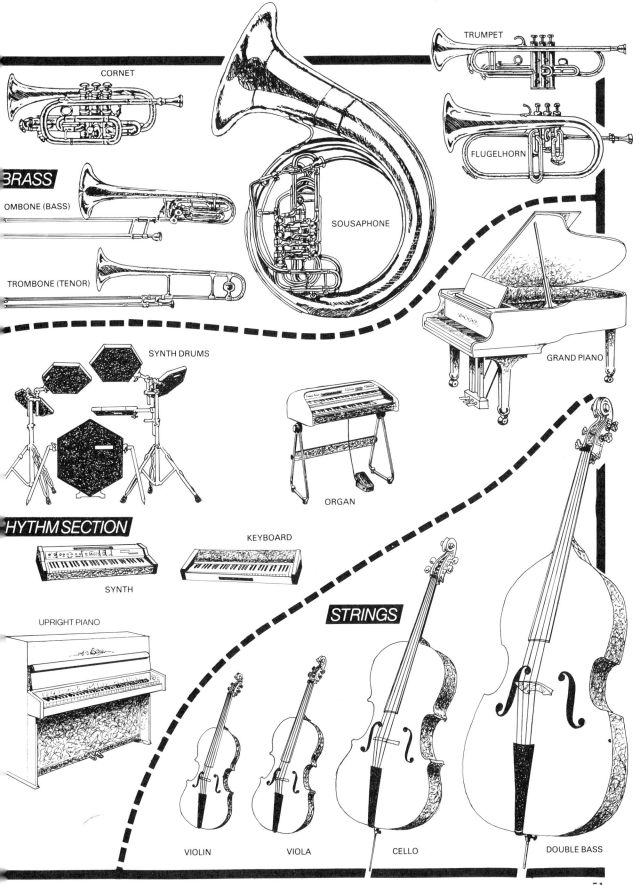

TRUMPET

CORNET

FLUGELHORN

BRASS

TROMBONE (BASS)

SOUSAPHONE

TROMBONE (TENOR)

GRAND PIANO

SYNTH DRUMS

ORGAN

RHYTHM SECTION

KEYBOARD

SYNTH

STRINGS

UPRIGHT PIANO

VIOLIN   VIOLA   CELLO   DOUBLE BASS

Basic guitar

Lots of people fancy the idea of playing electric guitar, but with a view to maintaining good relationships with family and neighbours an **acoustic** guitar is probably best to start with. As with most other things in life it's probably best not to buy the cheapest you can find. If possible, get someone who knows something about guitars to go with you when you buy one.

Acoustic guitar

Semi-acoustic electric guitar

Electric guitar

Bass guitar

The acoustic guitar shown here is probably the best to start with. It will have SIX strings, each tuned to a given note, and you can buy a set of **pitch pipes** like the ones pictured below, which will give you each note for tuning purposes. You'll need short fingernails on your left hand and slightly longer ones on your right hand – unless you want to play the guitar 'the other way round'. Choose a comfortable sitting position – a foot rest helps a lot. If you can read music you can begin straight away to play simple melodies – just picking out the tune, and when you've started to get control of your left hand you can then go on to play chords.

Some pieces of music will actually have the chord picture printed for you as well as the chord name:

but for others you'll have to memorize the finger positions for each chord. However, with just a few chords under your fingers you can play a great many tunes. You may find a **capo** is useful – it fits around the neck of the guitar and enables you to play in higher or lower pitched keys to make it more comfortable for your singing voice. You can play from most piano copies of light music because they'll have the chords written with the music, but if you want to become really skilful, keep up the practice of actually reading the notes and playing them so that you can play over tunes when you want to.

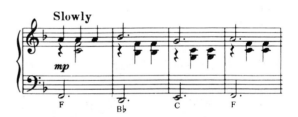

Guitar music usually shows **'strums'**, so 4 strums to a bar will be shown like this, with the chord name sometimes being used for the first strum – as in the second example here:

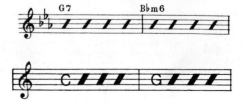

Clockwise, from left:
Jimi Hendrix;
John Williams;
Segovia;
Julian Bream;
Eric Clapton;
Jeff Beck.

The 12-string guitar is used in folk music and produces a thicker texture to accompany singing. The electric/acoustic guitar is common in jazz and is exactly what its name suggests.

The bass guitar is the electrified equivalent of the string double-bass and does not have an acoustic version. Again, with this instrument it is probably best to learn acoustically first, i.e. on the double-bass, although this instrument may well pose transport problems!

AMPLIFICATION

If you're a beginner on electric guitar or bass, get a small **practice combo** first, i.e. a piece of equipment that amplifies and plays the sound – it will be easier to carry and will play quietly enough to be used at home. Remember that you can always practise while using headphones and this can avoid a lot of family displeasure. It also means that people can't hear if you're not very good!

GUITAR CHORDS AND CHORD DIAGRAMS

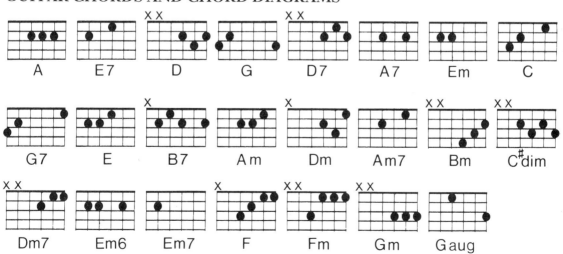

Basic keyboard

Many people can pick out a tune on the piano. Some people can only pick out the one at the bottom of the opposite page. A lot of people (such as old Uncle Jack or Aunty Mabel) play by ear.

So, what can you do?

Playing the piano properly is quite difficult – it means having regular lessons and doing regular practice. But anyone can pick out a tune, and with a bit of practice can put some chords with it. You may be lucky enough to have access to an electronic organ or micro keyboard or even a synthesizer and all these instruments make life easier for you.

THINGS TO DO

On any kind of keyboard try and pick out these tunes: any two Christmas carols; any two hymns; any two nursery rhymes; memories from *Cats*; 'Eastenders'; 'I'd Like to Teach the World to Sing'. It's probably easier to start the tunes on C, D, F or G, but any note will do.

LEARN TO PLAY CHORDS

1 Choose a white note, for example C.
2 Add the next but and the next but one again – E and G.
3 Play all three notes together. It's a chord of C major – C—E—G.
4 Spread the chord out, as shown by the arrows on the piano diagram.

On page 49 you can see how to get the right note with the right chord.

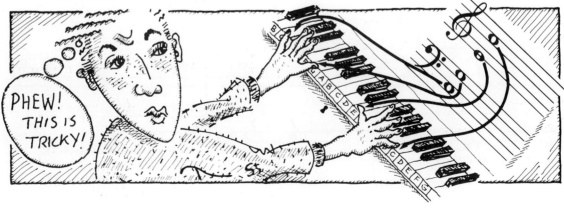

How many of these have you been lucky enough to have a go on? How many are there in your school?

Clockwise, from top left:
Upright piano; Hammond organ; spinet; church organ; clavichord; synthesizer; harmonium; harpsichord; concert grand piano.

Exercises to help you with your keyboard playing:

1 Try and use this hand position:
2 Rest your hand on a table and lift each finger, keeping the others still, to strengthen your finger muscles and develop independent control.
3 The old 5-finger exercise – corny, but it works.
4 Try to use more than one finger for playing.
5 Play with another instrument or something to help you keep the beat.
6 Try not to look at the keyboard.

Well – playing keyboards isn't easy, so don't give up too quickly. Keep coming back to it, and you should find that you gain control over your fingers the more often you practise. Good luck!

Jazzing a tune

Use this section in conjunction with *Jazz Improvisation* (page 12) and *Play Jazz* (page 28). The most immediately noticeable change that you can and should make is to the rhythm. It is important to feel this change of emphasis before you actually play.

Change this steady $\frac{4}{4}$ (4-beat rhythm):

into this slightly faster $\frac{4}{4}$:

Or this serious $\frac{3}{4}$ (3-beat rhythm):

into a jazz waltz:

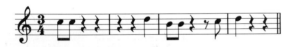

$\frac{6}{8}$ time can be played as if in $\frac{2}{4}$ or $\frac{4}{4}$ with ♩♪ ♩♪ rhythm – the following example should help.

Change this well-known tune:

into this 'swingy' number:

$\frac{3}{4}$ time can be easily changed to $\frac{4}{4}$, especially if a 'walking bass' is used.

Change this gentle, easy waltz tune:

into this 'swinging' feel:

WALKING BASS

In $\frac{4}{4}$ this involves playing one ♩ on each beat of the bar. So, take an easy given bass line and fill in the gaps as shown!

For example, a given part:

can be converted to:

Now, having dealt with the backing (the feel), let's look at the actual tune. Successful 'jazzing' will obviously depend on experience and there can be no hard or fast rules, but two elements are important. Firstly, the rhythmic aspect – altering the position of the accented note in the bar, like this:

Change this 'straight' tune:

to this:

And secondly, adding passing notes and certain extra notes – often referred to as 'blue notes':

Note: with all these rhythmic examples, the best way to understand them is to hear a demonstration of them being played – this will also help you to appreciate the difficulties involved in accurately writing them down.

Finally, here is an example for pianists who have perhaps got as far as Grade 5 standard. If you haven't and still fancy having a go, try it anyway.

A NOTE ABOUT RHYTHMIC NOTATION

Jazz/swing/light music has gradually acquired its own system for writing down the tricky rhythms which people seem able to play easily but not always to read! For example:

in 'swing' style would be played:

but 'rather inaccurately'!

Beginning of 'Lullaby of Birdland'
by George Shearing

Standard 32 (1)

This is a pattern that has been used by generations of song-writers, and the idea goes back several hundred years. It works like this:

Bars 1–8 are called	A	1	2	3	4	5	6	7	8
Bars 9–16 are called	A	9	10	11	12	13	14	15	16
Bars 17–24 are the middle eight	B	17	18	19	20	21	22	23	24
Bars 25–32 are a final repeat of section	A	25	26	27	28	29	30	31	32

So, you can see that the listener hears section A three times and the song-writer hopes that section A is the bit that will be remembered. From the 1930s to the 1960s the standard 32 has been the main pattern used by popular song-writers.

This section of the book gives you one to sing and play and in *Standard 32 (2)* on page 64 you'll have a chance to do a lot of the composition yourself! You may find that singing and playing this number is a little more difficult than some of the others in the book, because of its length, but work through it gently bit by bit, and you should manage quite well. It uses **bossa nova** rhythm!

(A) **Chords first**

(B)

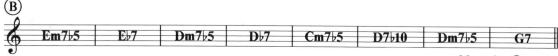

Now play (A) again.

The chords used written out

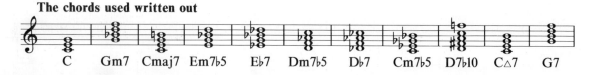

C   Gm7   Cmaj7   Em7♭5   E♭7   Dm7♭5   D♭7   Cm7♭5   D7♭10   C△7   G7

Tune (A) section

Now play (A) again.

58

(A) **Easy bass**

1/9/25 C	2/10/26 Gm7	3/11/27 C△7	4/12/28 C△7	5/13/29 C	6/14/30 Gm7	7/15/31 C△7	8/16/32 C△7

(B)

Em7b5 Eb7 Dm7b5 Db7 Cm7b5 D7b10 Dm7b5 G7

Now play (A) again.

(A) **Bb instruments**

(B)

Now play (A) again.

(A) **Glocks**

(B)

Now play (A) again.

(A) **Easy piano**

(B) **(Follow the same rhythm pattern.)**

Now play (A) again.

59

BOSSA NOVA RHYTHM

Bossa nova is a **'Latin-American'** rhythm. Don't worry about the name, concentrate on the patterns and enjoy it! The rhythm patterns are a little different to usual and make an interesting alternative, because with a little practice you can play a great many numbers 'Latin' style.

Bossa nova has 4 beats in a bar but you need to 'feel' all eight quavers:

The quavers are then regrouped in a 2-bar pattern:

You will find it easier to use the first bar from this pattern by itself to begin with. This gives you the bass pattern as used above. The other complication is that these bossa nova patterns are used in the rhythmic backings, so the tune cuts against them — thus providing further contrast.

Note: Bossa novas seem to attract 'tricky' chords, and the standard 32 on the previous page is no exception. Take them gently, and with your teacher's help you should be able to manage.

Reggae (1)

Reggae as a pop style is much misunderstood and condemned by many who have never tried to understand it. Although it often sounds simple and repetitive, it is quite difficult to master rhythmically. The basic unit is a 2-bar phrase:

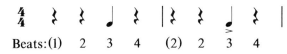

Beats: (1) 2 3 4 (2) 2 3 4

with an **accent** on the third beat of bar 2.

A simple way of building up a reggae sound is to use a selection of percussion instruments, as shown in the rhythm chart below, with the third beat accent being given to the bass drum, if possible. Piano or guitar chords will help to fill out the sound and the bass riff can be played on electric guitar or piano.

Use this section of the book to familiarize yourself with reggae rhythm and then use *Reggae (2)* (page 69) for a full reggae work-out. When you feel confident, have a go at writing a pop song in reggae style.

REGGAE RHYTHMS

WHAT TO DO

1 Learn the four rhythm patterns shown in the chart, either in small groups (4–6 people) or as a class.
2 Perform a vocal version first, using the silly words over the top – make sure you get the counting right.
3 Perform, using instruments.

Then, having got the rhythms sorted out we can now add some melody and harmony.

HARMONY

Try these chords:

Piano/glocks

Dm   G

with this bass riff:

Bb instruments (Clarinets/trumpets)

Add a tune – like this:

This is so ea-sy, it's simple, don't you think so?

and some words.

Cassettes

The cassette – or to give it its full title, the compact cassette – was pioneered by Phillips and came on the market in this country in 1964. The early cassettes had a playing time of 30 minutes per side (C60) and were sold blank; pre-recorded ones soon followed. The compact cassette came hard on the heels of the tape cartridge, which had been primarily intended for 'in-car' use, and had the great advantage over the cartridge of being 'rewindable'. A number of mechanical improvements concerning the way that the tape is handled inside the cassette have enabled it to reach very high standards, and various tape coatings have been experimented with to produce the best quality sound. However, perhaps the single most important advance in cassette quality is the introduction of the **Dolby** system, invented by an American, Dr Raymond Dolby. This system reduces the amount of tape hiss, which for many years held back sales of the cassette system. The turning point in sales terms came in 1970 when open-reel tape-recorder sales began to show a rapid decline against cassette-recorder sales figures.

Until the marketing of the **compact disc** (see page 63) the compact cassette has proved to be the most convenient and reliable form of recorded sound – for use at home, school, in the car and, of course, via portable machines. Playing time now ranges from the C30 to the C120. A Japanese experiment of marketing C180s in the mid-1970s proved unsuccessful, presumably because it is necessary to use very thin tape to provide for this length of recording time, and thinner tape is more likely to cause problems with static electricity which soon results in tape tangling and jamming.

Another advantage of cassettes is that home recording is made very easy and, of course, cassettes are much easier to store than long-playing discs. Only a tiny portion of tape at a given moment is in contact with the atmosphere, thus reducing the likelihood of dust damage or damage by mishandling.

A variety of different coatings are used for cassette tape and these can be identified from the labelled switches on many cassette players. Since their introduction, cassette players have gradually been upgraded in sound quality so that many listeners will gladly accept cassette sound quality as being as good as LP quality. However, it is unlikely that cassettes will ever surpass compact discs in sound quality.

The compact cassette.

Raymond Dolby.

CAN YOU?

1 Ask parents and teachers if they can remember life before cassettes. What advantages do they mention most about cassettes over records?
2 Make a survey at school to find out how many pupils have cassette players, and how many use a cassette with a computer.
3 Draw a diagram of a cassette, showing clearly how the tape is wound, and label each part.
4 Find out about and explain Dolby B, and Dolby C.

TALKING POINT

1 Why is 'small beautiful'? (Think of micro cassettes, 'Walkman', etc.)
2 Explain the reasons for the 'failure' of 8-track tapes.

Compact disc

To date, this is the latest development in the story of recorded sound. The success of the compact disc is difficult to assess at the moment, but it is certainly poised to be the successor to the LP – just as the LP took over from the 78 r.p.m. disc which in turn took over from the wax cylinder.

The compact disc came on to the market in 1982. It is unaffected by fingermarks and dust as there is no direct contact between the scanning mechanism and the disc surface – in simple terms, a compact disc cannot be easily damaged. Other advantages include the fact that the playing surface does not wear and the playing time is approximately one hour, uninterrupted.

Furthermore, the disc is digitally processed and carries more information on its surface than a conventional LP, thus giving much clearer and better sound-reproduction quality.

Compact discs also make finding particular points in the music easy as they can be scanned like a computer disc for information. Two other points that can be noted about its actual playing: the information is read from the middle outwards and as it appears from the underside.

CAN YOU?

1 Compare compact disc with your experience of computer technology.
2 Compare the role of a compact-disc owner today with that of a phonograph owner in 1890.
3 Find out how many compact discs are available to you locally.
4 Make a list or chart of ten stages in recording development from 1880 to 1990.
5 Draw a diagram of a compact disc, labelling any important features.
6 Write an argument against compact discs.

TALKING POINT

How much will compact disc progress be governed by price? (For example a system costs upwards of £200, and discs about £10 each at 1987 prices.)

Can there be further improvement? If so, suggest how.

A compact disc and player.

Standard 32 (2)

To remind you: a standard 32 is a pattern of 4 × 8 bars, A – A – B – A, which has been used a very great deal, especially in light and pop music. It's best to work through *Standard 32 (1)* first, on page 59.

A	1	2	3	4	5	6	7	8
A	9	10	11	12	13	14	15	16
B	17	18	19	20	21	22	23	24
A	25	26	27	28	29	30	31	32

This section gives you a standard 32 with various bits missing – add as much as you feel is necessary to make it a satisfying piece of music.

Chord pattern:

A	C	G	C	Am	Dm	G	C	G
A	"	"	"	"	"	"	"	C7
B	F	Fm	Em7	A7	Dm	Dm7	Gsus	G7
A	C	G	C	Am	Dm	G	C	C

Quite often the 'A' section is repeated using repeat signs and bars 15/16 may be shown as '2nd time' bars – look in the Rudiments section to see an example.

In this number the 'B' section uses the 'round the fifths' principle. Look in the Glossary for an explanation.

Chords used

C G Am Dm F Fm Em7 A7 Dm7 Gsus

TUNE

Make up your own tune using the notes from the chords. This is the most difficult part! Take as much time as you can get – don't reject any ideas, write them down or, if you can, put them on tape. Here are three sample openings:

RHYTHMIC BACKING

Use rock (page 35), bossa nova (page 60), reggae (page 61), or any other that you like or want to make up. You don't need to write it down other than for remembering purposes, so you can just use silly words to do this. It's best to practise the rhythms separately from the rest.

EASY BASS

For the simplest bass line, merely play the name note of the chord twice in each bar, like this:

You could then try a walking bass:

B♭ INSTRUMENTS

When you write for trumpets and clarinets you have to 'transpose' the music. It's very simple. If you want this note:

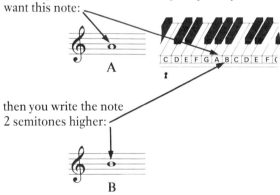

then you write the note 2 semitones higher:

You work out their part by choosing notes from the chords. For example, a sample beginning:

P.S. Ask your teacher about the key signature and look at the information on page 47 to remind you of transposing instruments.

The 1960s and the Beatles

There was skiffle, then rock 'n' roll, then a period of interest in **'trad. jazz'**, and then everything seemed to change in the 1960s. Pop music belonged to Britain in the 1960s – the so-called 'Swinging Sixties' – and perhaps for the first time Britain seemed to lead America in pop trends. Groups like the **Shadows** with **Cliff Richard** and singers like **Adam Faith** were at the forefront of pop music in 1960–1961, until a group called the **Beatles**, from Liverpool, appeared in 1961. By 1963 they had conquered the pop scene and with their individuality and musicianship made certain that it would never be the same again. Almost from the start they reacted against the fashions of rock 'n' roll and the middle-class fashions of the moment.

The Beatles in 1963.

Note: the hair un-greased and brushed forward; the very narrow trousers; the shoes with heels and the generally smart appearance.

LP sleeves of the early 1960s.

66

They used lead guitar, rhythm guitar, bass guitar and drums, and established a musical pattern in their line-up which was to be copied for years. They marked the final split from the style of pop music whose connections went back to the Swing era, and heralded the 'media' influence on pop. As with skiffle the idea of pop groups becoming 'respectable' via **'Tin-pan Alley'** – i.e. by becoming commercialized and thus acceptable to the older generation – can be seen to have happened to the Beatles. A great many other **Merseyside** groups developed in the early 1960s, like **Gerry and the Pacemakers, Freddy and the Dreamers,** and Britain led the pop world. The Beatles' chief rivals were the **Rolling Stones,** whose popularity stemmed to some extent from their ability to associate with rebellious youth and at the same time to alienate parents. Their long hair and seemingly sullen attitude produced adoring fans and outraged parents.

It is at this point that we begin to distinguish between 'kiddipop' – the Top Ten, and other pop – later to become recognized as the **'underground'** movement. It's important to remember, though, that many styles have gone 'underground' when they have faded from popularity, e.g. rock 'n' roll.

The next development is that of **Flower Power** when, in 1968, **San Francisco** (see map) became the temporary 'capital' of British pop. The ideas behind flower power – peace and love with no political viewpoint; an anti-materialist society; give someone a flower as a gesture of love and friendship – had reached England in 1966, led by

The Rolling Stones in 1964.

The Rolling Stones' first LP, released in 1964.

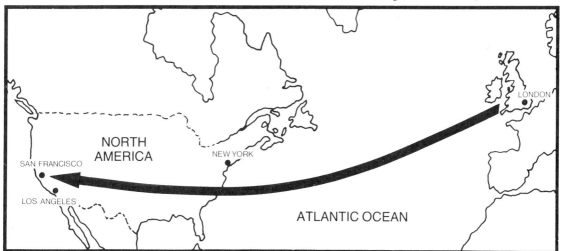

In the late 1960s, San Francisco became the 'temporary' capital of British pop.

the Beatles and the Rolling Stones who adopted these viewpoints. This movement also brought to the surface the drug culture that had always been connected with popular music and jazz. This was said to be apparent in songs such as 'Lucy in the Sky with Diamonds' by the Beatles – referring to LSD, widely used as a hallucinatory drug. Others said that that particular title was merely the name given to a picture that **John Lennon's** little son had brought home from school.

By the end of 1969 flower power had withered and died, but two things were established: firstly, that much 'hard' pop was anti-establishment, and secondly, the 'underground' movement now became established with the development of many groups catering specifically for its tastes. The period from 1957 to 1969 is perhaps the heydey of pop music in Britain, with the Beatles dominating it towards the end of that period.

CAN YOU?

1. Make a list of 1960s' groups.
2. Analyse one LP by the Beatles or the Rolling Stones and expain its success.
3. Compare 1960s' fashions with those of today, noting any similarities.
4. Compose a standard 32 in 1960s' style.
5. Give a performance of a 1960s' pop hit, but use only your ears to enable you to work out how it goes, i.e. by listening to the record.

TALKING POINT

What evidence is left of the 1960s' pop scene today in the form of places, buildings, clothes, music, people? What was the particular contribution of groups like the Who, that have not been mentioned here?

Where does the **BBC** and local radio fit into all this?

Reggae (2)

Use *Reggae (1)* (page 61) to familiarize yourself with reggae rhythms and then have a go at playing this reggae number. You may also find it helpful to use other sections in the book, for example, *Jazz Improvisation* (page 12).

The important thing with this reggae number is to try to get the 'feel' right. Once you have done that you can improvise – extend the tune; add a Ⓑ section, etc.

Bob Dylan

If we label the Sixties as 'swinging' – an apparent period of prosperity and particularly so in the pop world – then many would label the 1970s as depressing. It was a period of fragmentation in pop music where it is difficult to identify main dominating trends – everyone wanted to lead but could find nowhere to go.

Two leading pop figures died in 1970 – **Janis Joplin** and **Jimi Hendrix**; the Beatles broke up and **Simon and Garfunkel** went their own ways. All these pop stars represented very different styles and it perhaps seemed that they could no longer all survive side by side. It was as if the Seventies were waiting for an identifiable style to emerge in just the same way that rock 'n' roll appeared in the early 1950s, and the Beatles in the early 1960s – but no one style dominated in the 1970s. So we must aim to identify particular trends and it's perhaps relevant to look back at the 1960s and single out one particular person whose influence can be identified.

BOB DYLAN

Bob Dylan was born in 1941 and after an early interest in rock 'n' roll he became a fan of the American **Woody Guthrie** – a folk singer who influenced a great deal of American popular music.

Dylan's early songs were solos accompanied by his own guitar and blues harmonica – numbers like 'Blowin' in the Wind' and 'Masters of War' became immensely popular and were adopted by many young, left-wing people as sort of anthems. Dylan's attraction was perhaps that his music was raw, natural and thus in complete contrast to the increasingly studio-created sounds of other major groups. A second phase in Dylan's career involved a transition to being backed by an 'electric' rock band.

Meanwhile, back in the 1970s, some trends can be identified, such as:

1 The move to 'glamorous rock', e.g. **Sweet, Slade, Marc Bolan, Gary Glitter**.
2 'Ideal people', e.g. **The Osmonds, Jacksons, Monkees, David Cassidy, David Essex**.
3 The return of the solo star, e.g. **David Bowie, David Soul, Elton John, Rod Stewart**.
4 The girls, e.g. **Tammy Wynette, Dolly Parton, Melanie, Twiggy, Carly Simon, Olivia Newton-John, Elkie Brooks, Suzi Quatro**.

And, of course, we mustn't forget **Abba, Bob Marley, Stevie Wonder, Electric Light Orchestra, Roxy Music**, and many many more!

If a particular favourite of yours, or a particular style or trend has been left out, or if you've never heard of some of the names mentioned you'll appreciate the problem of any writer looking back at a recent period of history. If you feel strongly about it you will get a chance to air your views in a moment.

It becomes apparent, more than ever before, that in the 1970s listening choice was often made for a lot of people by the promoters of 'popular' music. Since the BBC first encountered problems with 'song-plugging' in the late 1920s, it has been well known that the public do respond to broadcast music and can easily be swayed to purchase a record that they have heard many times on the radio. This is only the tip of the iceberg – many other advertising and promotional methods are used by those in the pop industry (see page 78). Hence, a wide variety of pop styles can exist side by side, thanks to the fickle or catholic minded public – whichever way you look at it. Two other branches of pop music deserve individual attention in the 1970s: **Soul**, and **Punk**.

Clockwise from top left:
Suzi Quatro; Elkie Brooks; The Jackson Five; Rod
Stewart; The Monkees; Elton John; Gary Glitter; Sweet;
Bob Marley.

71

SOUL

A lasting movement in pop history with its origins in Black American music from the end of the last century, soul is as much a style of presentation, of feel and of mood, as of actual instrumentation or harmony. Its greatest flowering came in '60s' **Motown**, when **Berry Gordy** established in Detroit a 'training school' for black singers and instrumentalists, aiming at turning out a completely finished product. Great care and attention was given to 'personality', both on and off stage, and to personality presentation. Success came in the vast number of Motown hits, by names such as **Diana Ross**, the **Supremes**, Stevie Wonder, etc.

Clockwise from top right:
Marvin Gaye; Stevie Wonder; Diana Ross;
Gladys Knight and the Pips; Four Tops;
Martha and the Vandellas.

PUNK

This fairly short-lived movement in pop history has left its mark on a good deal of '80s' music – in just the same way that the outrageous Rolling Stones in the 1960s influenced a good many other bands. The **Sex Pistols** led the way and sought popularity by making themselves as unpopular as possible! Inevitably, punk could only last a short time, but its American version **'New Wave'** lent a sufficiently respectable aim to the movement to allow it to continue.

The 1980s and the generation of the micro-computer meant that another era of new styles was to begin. However, the 1970s produced a greater variety of pop sounds than perhaps any other period in the development of popular music.

Above: The Sex Pistols. Top left: The Tubes. Bottom left: The Damned.

CAN YOU?

1 Comment on the age of performers between 1920 and 1980 – why they always got younger.
2 Explain why you think punk is unacceptable to many.
3 Act out a scene between Ma, Pa, and 15-year-old daughter – the latter wants to go out with **Rat Scabies** from the **Damned**.
4 Make a list of all the 1970s' groups and individuals mentioned and check with a current pop paper to find out how many are still functioning.
5 Explain the position of Soul music in the modern pop world.

TALKING POINT

1 Did you and/or your parents listen to pop music in the 1970s? What were or are your favourites (or unfavourites)?
2 Are there any left-over influences in fashions and music from new wave or punk today?

Writing a pop song (1)

Well, you could just sit under a tree and wait for inspiration – Newton did all right, didn't he? But for most people it is easier to use a definite method like the one that follows.

THE HOOK

Most pop songs have a **hook** – it's just a short phrase or even just one word and it's the most memorable part of the song. Once you've got some ideas, try saying your hook against a regular pulse. Here are some examples:

Pulse	Jumpin' /	/	/	Jumpin' /	/	/	Jumpin' /	/	/
	1 2 3 4			1 2 3 4			1 2 3 4		

Pulse	Free and Ea - sy	Free and Ea - sy	Free and Ea - sy
	1 2 3 4	1 2 3 4	1 2 3 4

Pulse	Au - to - matic	Au - to - matic	Au - to - matic
	1 2 3 4	1 2 3 4	1 2 3 4

THE CHORUS

Before you start this bit you must decide the subject of your song. Yes – most pop songs are about LOVE, but yours doesn't have to be and you will usually find that the hook will fit in regardless. The **chorus** should be short and sweet with easy words to sing. It might include the hook or come immediately before it or after it. Once you've written the chorus, try saying it over a number of times – this will probably fix the rhythmic pattern of the words over the pulse and will probably help to suggest a tune.

TUNE FOR THE CHORUS

Begin by saying the words over. If this doesn't suggest a tune you will need to work with a melody instrument – glock, xylo, **metallophone**, or piano are probably best. Find a starting note and work from it. At this stage don't reject anything – you need all the ideas you can get! Either scribble down the names of the notes or use a stave or rely on a partner to remember the fragments that you make up. Then, try to string them together! Your teacher should be able to help you over this tricky bit.

THE VERSES

Most pop songs have at least three **verses**. The words can be more complicated than the chorus, but the lines don't have to rhyme. Verses usually give information or tell a story. Add a tune in the same way that you did for the chorus – it should have a little less interest than the chorus tune!

Pupils working on a music project.

ADDING BACKING

This will depend on how much you know about music – and whether, for example, you can play an instrument. This book will help you if you use the Index to find other sections that you may need.

Start by working out the rhythmic backing for claves, tambourine, cabasa, maracas, etc. Use a drum kit as well if there is one available, or a drum machine, then add simple glock parts – like the ones in this book in the sections titled *The 12-Bar Blues (1)*, and *Standard 32 (1)*.

You may also be able to add a simple piano part, perhaps with help from your teacher. Look at *The 12-Bar Blues (3)*, *Standard 32 (1)* and *Reggae (2)*.

TROUBLE SHOOTING HINTS

1 Getting started is always the most difficult bit. Don't reject *any* hook ideas – write them down and try saying them. It's better to work through a lot of ideas than be looking at a blank sheet of paper. If possible work with a tape or cassette recorder and keep all your ideas on that.
2 Chorus rhythm and tune – keep saying them over. Maybe one person in the group is better at doing tunes than the others – let him or her do the tune while you think about words and instruments.
3 Set yourself time limits. It's nearly always easier to work under a bit of pressure – and you can probably finish it at break or lunchtime or at home if you really get stuck.

Writing an advertising jingle

This is a bit like *Writing a Pop Song (1)* (page 74), but presents the composer with a different set of problems. You might find it helpful to do some research first, but if you're just itching to compose, jump on to the next section.

MARKET RESEARCH

It's probably best to work in a small group, say six of you, but you can work individually if you want to or as a whole class. Keep a note of your answers.

1 Make a list of your ten favourite advertisements – on television, radio or cinema – that you think effectively use music to promote their products.

2 From your list, pick out those which use specially made-up words or have a strong rhythmic pattern, for example:

BEAN(Z) MEAN(Z) HEINZ

Made-up words – to fit with *HEINZ*.

3 With the help of your teacher try to identify those advertisements that have had music specially written for them and those which have 'borrowed' (stolen?) music from composers. To help you start off, here are some examples – play them over.

Now hands that do di-shes can be soft as your face, with mild green Fair-y Li-quid.

Fairy Liquid – original

etc.

Hovis – 'borrowed' from the 'New World' Symphony by Dvořák

WRITING YOUR OWN JINGLE

Remember that, just as with *Writing a Pop Song (1)*, you need to follow the method – composing is not just a matter of waiting for inspiration, it's a question of working hard to produce good results.

METHOD

1 Choose your product:
   (a) One that already exists – but don't allow yourself to be influenced by any advertising music that's already been written for it.
   (b) A product of your imagination.
   (c) A 'home-made' product – maybe Mum's cooking (or Dad's cooking!).
   (d) Something really silly.

2 Make up the slogan:
   This is the difficult bit – like writing a good hook for a song. WORDS first, then the tune – strong rhythmic interest helps, as do 'English devices' like alliteration. Here are some interesting slogans to help you think:

   * * * * for Glue   'A small deposit secures any article'
   * * * * for Sausages   'PORKY and BEST'
   * * * * for Beer   'Refreshes the parts', etc.

3 Completing the rest of the advertisement:
   Most advertisements are quite short because television time is very expensive to buy – 30 seconds is quite a suitable amount of time to aim for. Your advertisement will include the slogan as part of a chorus, probably 3 or 4 lines at the most – all product centred. In other words, keep to the point – don't waffle – time is money!

4 Scripting:
   It's fun to make a complete advertisement, which may include some dialogue, and you can also decide what shots the camera will make and when the music will start and stop. A simple script is shown below. Finally, try to make a recording (possibly a video?) of your advertisement. It's interesting to compare yours with those of the others in your group and discuss which ones you consider most effective and why.

Sample script

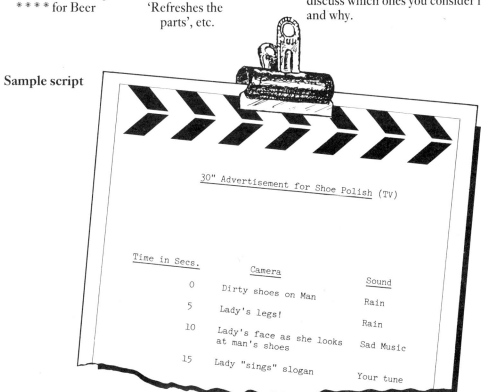

30" Advertisement for Shoe Polish (TV)

Time in Secs.	Camera	Sound
0	Dirty shoes on Man	Rain
5	Lady's legs!	Rain
10	Lady's face as she looks at man's shoes	Sad Music
15	Lady "sings" slogan	Your tune

The 1980s

It's always difficult to write, talk, or even think about what has happened recently, or what is happening now – ask your history teacher! Perhaps the only effective way to do it is to write our opinions of today's music and then refer to it in, say, five, ten or twenty years' time. Whatever we think or feel like now, it is likely that our opinions will change as time goes by. However, let's try to identify some characteristics that are noticeable about pop music in the 1980s.

PROMOTION OF POP MUSIC

In the 1980s the pop video has come into its own. Even though this method of selling pop records dates back to 1964 with the **Moody Blues'** 'Go Now', its effectiveness was restricted to the number of people owning videos. In the 1980s, video prices have come down – many homes now have one, and an ever-increasing number of pubs have included videos as part of their entertainment facilities. **Adam Ant** is a perfect example of a pop star who used video to sell his product in a highly efficient manner – creating a new character for each video, rather like **David Bowie** had done in the 1970s. Many other groups use video as the '80s progress, and the more noticeable their name the more likely they are to succeed; for example: **Bananarama, Kid Creole and the Cocoanuts, Dépêche Mode, Echo and the Bunnymen, Wham!**, etc.

GROUP IMAGES

The 1980s has produced a predominance of neat and tidy groups – in other words, groups who have cared about their appearance and grooming. Even though the appearance may have shocked parents (**Boy George**, for instance), the older generation always takes note of pride in appearance. This style is in sharp reaction to punk which emphasized untidiness and anti-social characteristics. Glamour also provided stark contrast to unemployment – a problem for many people, both young and old. Groups like **Police** and **Duran Duran** have followed a similar pattern of success to the Beatles, including visits to America.

This page, top to bottom:
Mel & Kim, Siouxsie Sioux; Adam Ant; Madonna.

Opposite page, clockwise:
Simply Red; Five Star; Spandau Ballet; Level 42; Curiosity Killed the Cat; Freddie Mercury of Queen; Boy George; UB 40; A-Ha.

WHAT NOW – WHAT NEXT?

You the reader must complete this section!

At this moment the 1980s seems like a complicated mixture of styles and there doesn't seem to be one dominating style, but perhaps when we look back in thirty or more years' time it will all seem much simpler – over to you.

CAN YOU?

1 List as many pop groups as you can, with a brief description of their musical style.
2 Find out as much as you can about the favourite pop music of someone over thirty (a parent, friend, teacher) when they were your age – how have things changed?
3 Suggest a future for pop music. What part will electronics play? Are human beings out?

TALKING POINT

After videos, what next? What will pop promoters turn to?

Writing a pop song (2)

In *Writing a Pop Song (1)* (page 74), we experimented with a method which involved starting from scratch, as this usually leads to a satisfying result. In this section we are going to start with some given words. Most 'classical' composers worked in this way, but don't be put off by that. You could write your own words or choose any text you like – perhaps your English teacher could help you with this, but don't worry, you won't have to spend hours reading poetry books if you don't want to.

Here are two sample texts:

1 Lady at the window
  Widow of the war
  Staring at brown photographs
  Through an **open door**

2 **Dark nights** all alone
  Feeling lonely on my own
  Do you still **remember me**
  Am I just part of your history?

Words in bold = possible hooks

METHOD

The next bit is much the same as *Writing a Pop Song (1)*, except that you need to take a word or phrase, or add your own word or phrase, in order to create a hook. Keep reading the words through – out loud – perhaps with other people, so that the rhythm patterns begin to suggest themselves. The mood created by the words should help to suggest tempo and feel. The words in **bold** are possible hook words and the given bit could be a chorus or you may use it as a verse and compose your own chorus. In other words, it's a very flexible method, because you're working like a real composer – from scratch!!

It's a good idea to keep a note of all your ideas, on paper or on tape if you can – don't reject anything at this stage.

DECORATION – RHYTHM

Certain words may suggest a stronger rhythm idea, for example:

or:

There are endless possibilities and the best way is probably to experiment using a melody instrument, for example, flute, clarinet, violin, piano, etc.

As with so much practical music it will be ideal if you can work in a small group in your own space; but if not, try to work purposefully and quietly in your own part of the classroom. The more effort you put in, the more you'll get from it.

CHORD PATTERNS

A strong feature of a song can be a chord pattern as, for example, in 'The House of the Rising Sun':

Am	C	D	F	Am	E	Am	E

or 'Light my Fire':

Bbm7	Gm7	Bbm7	Gm7

and you may be able to insert a strong chordal section, or use it as chorus backing, or for an intro, which can help to make a song hold together. As with so many compositional features, the best way to find out is to experiment for yourself.

TESTING

As soon as you can, make a rough tape recording of your composition and try it out on classmates. Their reaction can be a most helpful form of criticism because they'll be hearing the piece for the first time, whereas you have become accustomed to it. Try to make a note of their opinions and then alter things if you think that their criticism was justified.

Making a demo

For many of you the idea of making a professional standard recording will be an important goal and for some it will be an essential part of your career plan. While it may not be possible, physically or financially, for all of you to go into a recording studio, it seems like a good idea to have this sort of recording standard as a target to work towards.

Some of you will be fortunate to have a sufficiently well-equipped music department in your school to enable you to produce high-quality recordings. Here, no doubt, the biggest pressure will be the restriction on time – the fact that there will always be others queueing up to use the equipment and that you will always have other lessons to go to. However, this in itself provides an important learning point because, if you go to a professional studio you will be up against the problem of 'time equals money'. So, many of the remarks in this section can apply equally well to organizing a recording session at school or in a studio.

PLANNING

Make sure that you know why you are making the recording. Here are some possible reasons:

* making a demo, to get gigs for your band
* for fun
* to gain experience
* school exam work.

Whatever the reason, you need to know because it will help to determine the degree of quality that you're expecting, and that's important because it governs everything else.

MUSICAL PLANNING

You and/or your group must be well practised and familiar with your sound on an ordinary tape recorder. A recording session should not and often cannot afford to be a practice session. Decide exactly which numbers you want to get on tape at which session. Don't fall into the trap of: 'Oh, we've got twenty minutes left, let's just play so-and-so as well.' It's important that each member of the group can sing or play his or her bit on their own.

A recording studio at Air Studios. London.

EQUIPMENT PLANNING

Make sure that you are completely familiar with the musical and technical facility of your own equipment and that of the studio. There's nothing worse than your synth. player being unable to produce a particular sound, or saying, 'What about this,' etc. All the experimental stuff should be done in practice sessions beforehand. Make sure that all your equipment works and that you have all the necessary leads. Guitar strings need to be of good quality – replace if necessary, but not on the day of the recording.

TUNING

Even if you don't bother much normally, out of tune playing will really show up on a recording, so ensure that:
(a) each person can play his or her bit in tune, and
(b) you know how to tune each instrument or voice. An electronic tuner can work wonders – but make sure that you know how to use it.

THE RECORDING ENGINEER

If it's a professional studio you must meet the engineer and talk through your session with him some time before the recording date. He can advise you on equipment, use of studio equipment, the way to set up in the studio, and the number of recording tracks that he thinks you'll need. Remember that he's probably got a lot more experience than you have. If it's a recording session at school you still need a 'recording engineer' – it's almost impossible to be in charge of the recording session and to play and sing as well.

THE STUDIO

Be it professional or school: GET ORGANIZED, so that you can get in quickly, set up quickly, put cases out of the way, and be ready to play as soon as possible. Place a ban on 'practising', 'showing-off'. Check tuning and levels and record in accordance with the plan that you worked out with the engineer beforehand. If a professional engineer offers advice, take it. Try to avoid doing silly things, such as tapping your foot against the mike stand, or swaying away from the mike when you're singing.

MIXING

After the recording comes the most important part. Don't be tempted into adding all sorts of special effects if you're in a professional studio – they simply sound like studio effects. Again, follow the engineer's advice.

VOCALS

You need to practise just as much as the instrumentalists and you will probably benefit most of all if you make sure you're not in any smoky, stuffy rooms – plenty of fresh air and drinking only water and soft drinks will help before and during a recording session. If it helps, wear your stage clothes during the recording.

FINALLY

After you've made the recording, come back to it fresh a day or so later and criticize it constructively, noting good points, bad points, and room for improvement in all departments – technical matters; musical proficiency; composition, etc. Listen to and take note of criticism from others as well – it's the only way to get better.

The rhythmic idea

The final two sections in this book deal with two more aspects of composition. To be an effective composer usually means to be competent in handling a variety of techniques and being able to add to those techniques your own 'certain something'. This book has looked at points of technique in connection with certain styles – those connected with 'popular' music – and these two final sections may provide a stepping stone to a more thorough study of 'harmony', which will lay an essential foundation for further composition work.

Anyway, let's get on with it! We've already mentioned, on page 80, the idea of chordal patterns, and the three elements of *harmony*, *rhythm*, and *melody* are all closely interwoven. Some popular songs have been successful because they have a frequently repeated rhythm pattern which itself acts as a hook. It's almost as if you can hang any chordal pattern or melody onto that rhythm and it doesn't matter because it's the rhythm that gets noticed.

Have a look at these examples – play them over, or have them played to you and if possible listen to a recording of the piece.

1 'It don't mean a thing (if it ain't got that swing)', written by Duke Ellington in 1932.

It's the 'doo-wah' bit that is the memorable rhythmic chunk of this number.
It's been reissued many times and been in the Top Ten quite recently!

2 'When I'm Sixty-four', composed by John Lennon and Paul McCartney.

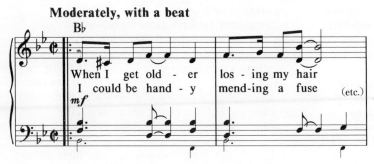

This opening rhythm predominates throughout the song.

3 'Can't smile without you', recorded by Barry Manilow.

This rhythm used in the introduction is also used frequently in the backing throughout the song.

Think on these matters, please:

1 You may not like these songs.

2 You may not like the performers of these songs.

3 The songs and their performers have been successful.

4 The composer must communicate with his audience.

Now it's your turn. Here are some ways of
establishing rhythmic patterns:

1 Work in pairs. One person claps 4 beats in a bar,
   rests for two bars and repeats. The other claps an
   original pattern in the two empty bars:

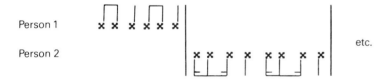

2 Question and answer – again work in pairs. One
   claps a short rhythmic phrase and the other tries
   to provide a satisfactory answer so that the whole
   thing makes one rhythmic phrase:

3 Steal rhythms from any source that you can –
   alter them slightly so that you can claim the
   credit!

4 Examine some other very rhythmic composers,
   for example: Stravinsky – ask your teacher to
   play you some examples; **Don Ellis** – a modern
   American musician and composer who employed
   very unusual time signatures. Ask your teacher to
   get hold of some examples for you.

The melodic idea

This links with the previous section and is a
composition technique that is quite fashionable
amongst 'serious' composers today. The idea is to
develop a simple melody and repeat it many times –
both harmonic, i.e. chordal support, and rhythmic
strength are of secondary importance. Let's begin
by looking at some effective examples.

1 'Für Elise', by Beethoven

This is one of those bits of Beethoven that lots of
people can play and although it has a strong
harmonic sense it's the pattern of notes that counts.

2 'Morning' from *Peer Gynt* by Grieg

Again there is a strong harmonic sense, but the
pattern of notes creates the mood.

3 Here's an example of an original idea that's so
good it has been borrowed by many composers
including Brahms, Liszt and Rachmaninov.
Where would Andrew Lloyd-Webber's 'South
Bank Show' tune 'Variations' be without such a
marvellous theme as Paganini's to build on?

And now, you must have a go at creating some
patterns like these, and you may well find that this
is one of the most difficult tasks in the book and
particularly difficult to do in a busy classroom. So,
perhaps this is one piece of work to be done alone -
at school, or at home - and preferably with the help
of a melody instrument. As with all composition
tasks, reject nothing – put all your ideas on tape or
on paper, so that you can listen to them afterwards
and select objectively. It's the only way to succeed.

In conclusion

It is hoped that this book has helped to encourage you to be a practical musician, whether composer or performer, and has involved you in some constructive listening as well. A great deal of composition can be successfully achieved with a fairly small amount of musical knowledge. There will come a point from which, in order to go further, you will need to make a formal study of harmony. Don't despise or reject this, even though it may mean spending some time composing in a style to which you are not attracted. Remember that nearly all composers and song-writers have had to go through this and it will open a great many doors for you. There's nothing to stop you composing in popular styles at the same time and your increased harmonic knowledge should increase the interest of your compositions considerably. Lastly, remember that you are a communicator – SPEAK CLEARLY!

Discography

Any discography is a dangerous thing – you may spend hours trying to get hold of one record which isn't the best example of something, or you find that you've heard it already, or it's been deleted and is only available in Baluchistan.

So, here's a list of listening suggestions in chronological order, with – in the right-hand column – some composers/performers who can be linked with a particular period or style. Use this list for listening ideas and/or as a starting point for research into a particular period or style. Cross-refer to the glossary (pages 38–41) for more information.

1920s	Paul Whiteman Bix Beiderbecke
1930s	George Gershwin Any 78 r.p.m. records – for sound quality Duke Ellington Count Basie Benny Goodman The Dorsey brothers
1940s	Stan Kenton Buddy Rich Louis Armstrong Tin Roof Blues **Oklahoma.**
1950s	Lonnie Donegan Tommy Steele Bill Haley Elvis Presley Buddy Holly Everly Brothers Cliff Richard
1960s	Beatles Rolling Stones Gerry and the Pacemakers Freddy and the Dreamers
1970s	Jimi Hendrix Janis Joplin Bob Dylan Gary Glitter Osmonds Abba Diana Ross Stevie Wonder
1980s	TV adverts Wham! Echo and the Bunnymen Adam Ant Police

Elgar, e.g. *Enigma Variations*
Richard Strauss, e.g. any of the Tone Poems
Ravel, e.g. *Bolero*
Stravinsky, e.g. his ballet music
Beethoven, e.g. his symphonies
Don Ellis, e.g. *Electric Bath*
George Shearing, e.g. any piano solos
Gil Evans, e.g. *Miles Ahead*
Jarré, e.g. *Equinox*
Swingle II, e.g. *Madrigals*
King's Singers, e.g. *Contemporary Collection*
The Singers Unlimited, e.g. *A cappella*

List of books and addresses

If you want to find out more about popular music and musicians, the following books will help:

The Dance Band Era by Albert McCarthy (Studio Vista)
The Gramophone Guide to Hi-Fi by John Borwick (David & Charles)
Guinness Book of Recorded Sound (Guinness Books)
Guinness Book Hit Singles (Guinness Books)
The Illustrated History of Rock Music by Jeremy Pascall (Hamlyn)
The Making of Jazz by James Lincoln Collier (Papermac)
Musical Instruments of the World (originally pub. Paddington Press; now available from Omnibus Press)
New Grove Dictionary of Music and Musicians (Macmillan)
Who's Who of Jazz by John Chilton (Papermac)

Where to get music and arrangements from:

Belwin-Mills Music Ltd, 250 Purley Way, Croydon, Surrey CR9 4QD
Boosey & Hawkes Music Publishers Ltd, The Hyde, Edgware Road, London NW9 6JN
Capital Music Centre, 64 Dean Street, London W1V 5HG
Chappell Music Ltd, 129 Park Street, London W1Y 3FA
Chester Music, 7–9 Eagle Court, London EC1M 5QD
EMI Music Publishing Ltd, 138–140 Charing Cross Road, London WC2H 0LD
International Music Publications, Southend Road, Woodford Green, Essex IG8 8HN
Jazzwise Publications, 13 Foulser Road, London SW17 8UE
London Orchestrations, 45 Norman Avenue, Sanderstead, South Croydon, Surrey CR2 0QH
Music Sales Ltd, 78 Newman Street, London W1P 3LA
Oxford University Press (Music Department), 119–125 Wardour Street, London W1V 4DN
Studio Music Company, 77–79 Dudden Hill Lane, London NW10 1BD.

For more addresses and information on many useful music sources, the following books will help:

British Music Education Yearbook and *British Music Yearbook*, (both published by Rhinegold Publishing)

Assessment

You and your music teacher may wish to use this part of the book to help assess and mark your work and progress.

You can be marked on written work, aural contribution, performance and composition. The only person you really compete with is yourself – so see if you can do your best and where possible show an improvement. Follow the marking scheme opposite and mark each piece of work that you complete in three ways:

1 your own marks;
2 your classmates' mark of your work;
3 your teacher's mark.

PAGE	SECTION	Written	Aural	Perf.	Comp	Teacher's Grade	Teacher's Comment	Date
	Popular music in Britain at the beginning of this century							
	Jazz improvisation							
	The 12-bar blues (1)	3 C	– –	2 B	3 D			
	Riffs and easy figures							
	Acoustic and electrical recording							
	Big Bands							
	Adding thirds							
	Plastic discs and LP presentation							
	Play jazz on your . . .							
	Skiffle and rock 'n' roll							
	The 12-bar blues (2)							
	The 12-bar blues (3) – jazz							
	Chords for pop and jazz	2 C	2 C	– –	– –			
	Basic guitar							
	Basic keyboard							
	Jazzing a tune							
	Standard 32 (1)							
	Reggae (1)							
	Cassettes							
	Compact disc							
	Standard 32 (2)							
	The 1960s and the Beatles							
	Reggae (2)							
	The 1970s							
	Writing a pop song (1)							
	Writing an advertising jingle							
	The 1980s							
	Writing a pop song (2)							
	Making a demo							
	The rhythmic idea							
	The melodic idea							

MARKING SCHEME

Personal application

1 Applies him/herself with exceptional diligence.
2 Can be relied upon to do his/her best.
3 Generally does his/her best.
4 Generally makes no more than the minimum effort.
5 Effort inconsistent.
6 Serious lack of effort.

Attainment

A Excellent.
B Has a good grasp of the skills involved.
C Has a reasonable grasp of skills.
D Has a limited grasp of skills.
E Has a serious problem with the work.

Teacher's grade

The teacher's grade should be based on the marking scheme suggested by the examination group. It may be helpful to use the marking scheme above for continuous assessment.

Index